SHARM EL-SHEI

DIVING GUIDE

SWAN·HILL
PRESS

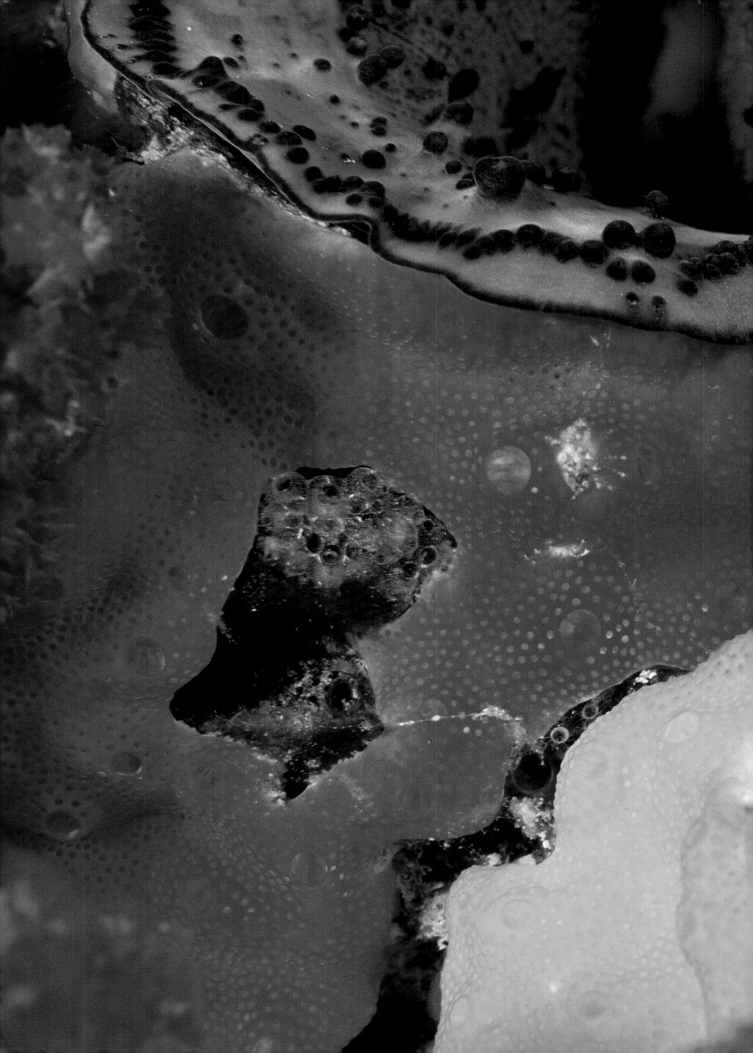

1 Colourful cascades of alcyonarians tumble from the reef's walls, giving the floor of the Red Sea its own special charm.

2-3 Brilliant colors are characteristic of the sea floor at Sharm el-Sheikh. In this area, corals seem to compete with each other to offer the brightest colors: bright red and yellow encrusting sponges have colonized the valves of this blue-mantled giant clam.

4 top Dense schools of fusiliers (Caesio suevica) swim along the vertical walls of the coral reef.

4 bottom This turkeyfish (Pterois miles) dances in all its splendor, brushing the fans of a gorgonian.

SHARM EL-SHEIKH
DIVING GUIDE

Text and photographs
Claudio Cangini

Graphic design
Clara Zanotti

Translation
Studio Traduzioni Vecchia, Milan

Illustrations of the dives
Cristina Franco

Fish charts

Texts
Angelo Mojetta
Illustrations
Monica Falcone

Contents

EGYPT

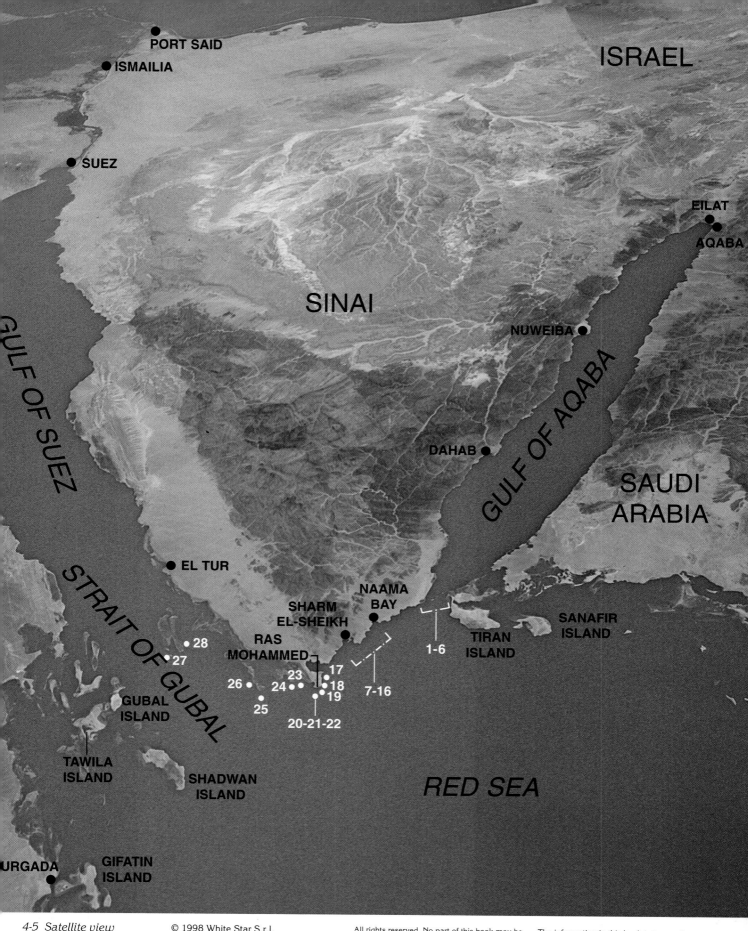

PORT SAID

ISMAILIA

ISRAEL

SUEZ

EILAT

AQABA

SINAI

GULF OF SUEZ

NUWEIBA

GULF OF AQABA

DAHAB

SAUDI
ARABIA

EL TUR

STRAIT OF GUBAL

NAAMA
BAY

SHARM
EL-SHEIKH

SANAFIR
ISLAND

28

RAS
MOHAMMED

1-6

TIRAN
ISLAND

27

17

26

23

24

18

7-16

25

19

GUBAL
ISLAND

20-21-22

TAWILA
ISLAND

SHADWAN
ISLAND

RED SEA

URGADA

GIFATIN
ISLAND

*4-5 Satellite view
of the Sinai
peninsula.*
Photograph
by NASA

© 1998 White Star S.r.l.
First Published in the UK in 1998
by Swan Hill Press, an imprint
of Airlife Publishing Ltd

British Library Cataloguing in Publication Data
A catalogue record for this book is available
from the British Library

ISBN 1 84037 036 X

The information in this book is true and
complete to the best of our knowledge.
All recommendations are made without
any guarantee on the part of the publisher,
who also disclaims any liability incurred
in connection with the use of this data
or specific details.

INTRODUCTION

Ever since scuba divers discovered it in the 1950s, the Red Sea has been considered the most beautiful and colorful sea in the world. A tropical sea, its temperature never goes below 22°C. This, along with its very salty waters, has made it an exceptional biological environment with sea beds of legendary beauty. Because it is a closed sea with no rivers running into it, the Red Sea is one of the clearest and most transparent seas on the planet, and light filters down to great depths. The greatest attraction for snorkelers and scuba divers is certainly the coral reef, which in this area is known as the barrier reef. This fragile ecosystem provides shelter and nourishment for thousands of organisms which coexist within a complex food chain. Different defense systems and feeding strategies have permitted various organisms to share the same area.
All these organisms have the same goals for survival: occupy a territory and defend it, eat, and reproduce under optimal conditions to ensure the continuity of the species. If any of these objectives is not reached, the species will disappear from the reef.
The fragile world of corals is constantly changing. Stony corals work constantly to build up the reef, which is then crumbled and changed by the animals that feed on it. If the reef is damaged by outside factors, its complex equilibrium is irremediably changed, with dramatic consequences.
The authorities of Sharm el-Sheikh, well aware of these possible alterations caused by human impact, have created a series of regulations and protected areas which have made the Sinai coast the best protected area of the Egyptian Red Sea.
In 1983, the need to protect this extraordinary environment led to the creation of the Ras Mohammed

A - An aerial view of the cape of Ras Mohammed shows the long inlet of Hidden Bay in the foreground, with Mangrove Channel to the left, separating Mangrove Island from the mainland.

B - The high buttresses of Shark Observatory are a spectacular observation point for the coast. Its sheer walls plunging down below the water's surface can be explored in fascinating underwater excursions.

C - The deep bay of Sharm el-Maya offers shelter for the night for all diving boats operating in the area. The mountains behind the inlet protect the bay from the wind. There are several hotels on the beach next to the pier.

National Park, which in 1989 was extended to other areas. Today the protected areas in the South Sinai cover an area 11,000 square kilometers in size. The protected areas include coral reefs, high mountain deserts, coastal lagoons and important cultural and religious areas. The coastal areas are constantly monitored by a staff of marine biologists who check the state of health of the reef and its fantastic inhabitants, while a group of rangers in the interior sees that park regulations are observed in those areas.

Sharm el-Sheikh is on the eastern side of the Sinai Peninsula, right in the center of this oasis that has benefited from the establishment of the park. The tourist district consists of two areas: the first is Sharm el-Sheikh, a small town built in 1968 that overlooks the Sharm el-Maya Bay and has a vacation port, a handful of hotels, typical eating places where you can try out the local cuisine, and a picturesque bazaar where you can buy hand-crafted products. Six kilometers to the north is the splendid Naama Bay,

D - Gorgonian sea fans reach their maximum dimensions in this part of the Red Sea. In areas swept by currents, it is not uncommon to see true forests of these sea fans with their horny skeletons, which join together to cover dozens of square meters of reef.

E - There are always large groups of pelagic fish like these bigeye trevallies (Caranx sexfasciatus) in areas that stretch out to the open sea. Because they are predators, these fish always swim near the reef in search of food, but their most successful attacks only come at dusk.

F - The large schools of batfish are always a fascinating sight. There are two species in the Red Sea (Platax orbicularis and Platax teira). These fish with their curious disk shape are not disturbed by divers, even when they come quite close.

G - The vertical walls that characterize the underwater area of the southern Sinai are swept by constant currents that carry in nutrition and guarantee the corals extraordinarily luxuriant growth. The floor of the Red Sea is considered one of the most spectacular sea beds in the world.

the real vacation center of the Sinai, where there are large hotels, shopping centers, banks and all the other infrastructures necessary for a vacation area. The seaside promenade along Naama beach is lined with date palms, and there are elegant restaurants and typical open-air cafes. There are also discotheques to enliven the evenings for more fun-loving types, and a casino where you can try out your luck.

A vacation at Sharm el-Sheikh is thus not just for scuba divers, and even their non-diving companions will find such a vast array of services and land excursions that they will never be bored. Over recent years, Sharm el-Sheikh has experienced a significant increase in tourism, encouraged by its moderate prices

and proximity to Europe (it is only four hours away from any part of Europe on one of the numerous charter flights).

Despite the crowds, the fascination of what can be described as "our tropical sea" continues, and the sea of Sharm el-Sheikh still holds more treasures than you can possibly discover in a week of scuba dives. This is why its waters are so beloved to scuba divers the world over, and why they enthusiastically return to visit it year after year.

E

F

D

G

THE DIVES

There are dozens of diving areas around Sharm el-Sheikh, each one different and capable of meeting the needs of all types of scuba divers, from neophytes to experts. Despite the fact that the area is visited by many divers, the protection policies of the government and the diving centers have kept the sea beds in excellent condition.

In many areas there are permanent mooring lines where diving boats can be tied (a maximum of four per line). These buoys, known in Egyptian as *shamandura*, have eliminated the need to drop anchors onto the reef, thus protecting the corals. Four to five square meters of the upper portion of the submerged reef could be damaged every time a boat drops and pulls anchor: this never happens at Sharm el-Sheikh!

In areas where there are no lines, scuba divers use drift dive techniques, with the boat in movement following the divers from the surface, picking them up at the end of the dive. The boats used by the diving centers for daily excursions are comfortable motor yachts from 15 to 20 meters long, built especially for scuba diving. The stern has a spacious cockpit with room for tanks and equipment, where divers can be comfortably seated as they dress, while a wide platform makes it easy to enter the water. A tasty lunch prepared in the galley on board can be enjoyed between one dive and another as you sit peacefully on the sofas in the dinette. Ample room for sunbathing and relaxing is located at the bow and on the upper sundeck. Usually boats with scuba divers on board depart at about 9:00 a.m. from two landing stages at Sharm el-Maya and Naama Bay and return in the afternoon after two or three dives. The area has excellent service from numerous diving centers with high quality staff sensitive to all the problems of environmental protection. During briefing, your

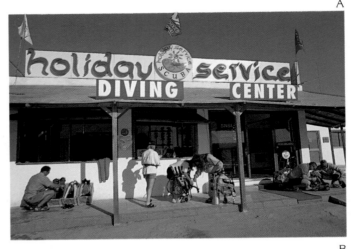

A

B

C

A - Holiday Service is one of the best-qualified diving centers at Sharm el-Sheikh. The instructors and underwater guides who work at the more professional diving centers in the area are fully qualified and will organize and handle your dives with expert care.

B - The Holiday 1, a fast boat designed and built especially for divers. The stern has a spacious cockpit with room for tanks and equipment, where divers can sit comfortably as they dress. The convenient sundeck provides a relaxing break between dives.

C - A cruise could be a pleasant way to enjoy a diving vacation, giving the most demanding divers the opportunity to reach sea beds of surprising beauty.

D - With scuba diving's rapid growth over recent years, new ways of diving have developed. The first innovation for recreational diving was an enriched oxygen mixture known as Nitrox, which allows divers to stay under longer and minimizes any problems caused by breathing compressed air. The latest frontier is certainly diving with semi-closed breathing systems. The advantages of these simple devices are endless and provide greater autonomy, allowing divers to explore the sea bed without making bubbles, thus enabling them to approach even the more timid fish who are sensitive to the noise a normal tank makes.

guides or instructors will repeatedly tell you to be extremely careful while you are in the water so as not to damage the sea bed. Some diving centers especially attentive to market development and trends now have equipment that allows you to dive using air mixtures enriched with oxygen, commonly called Nitrox. Nitrox is simply a breathing mixture with a 21% oxygen content, higher than normal, which makes it possible to stay underwater longer than with simple air. The consequent advantage is that the lower level of nitrogen in Nitrox resolves the problems divers experience when breathing nitrogen under pressure. SNSI (Scuba Nitrox Safety International), an educational

agency which produces Nitrox training systems, has its Egyptian offices in Naama Bay at the Holiday Service diving center, where you can also find "Rebreathers," closed and semi-closed circuit breathing systems where divers surface without creating bubbles, a great advantage for underwater photographers, who can thus approach their "prey" without frightening them.

E

F

G

E - The Ras um Sid area offers a classic example of the reef conformation typical of the Red Sea. Starting from the coastline, there is a belt of corals running parallel to the coast. It may emerge in some areas, while the portion facing the sea plunges down in nearly vertical walls.

F - The absolute ban on dropping anchors onto the reef has preserved the sea beds, and the delicate ecosystem of the coral reef, unlike other areas of the Egyptian Red Sea, is in excellent health. This tropical sea so close to Europe certainly offers marvelous diving opportunities for divers with any degree of experience.

G - Dives are always at a maximum depth of 30 meters, as this is where corals reach their maximum splendor. The exceptional transparency of the water and the always pleasant climate make a trip to this part of the Red Sea enjoyable at any time of the year. You can dive in these waters all year round without problems.

DIVING SITES

The diving areas that can be reached from Sharm el-Sheikh can be divided into four large areas, each of which has different features:

● **The Strait of Tiran.**
● **Local dives.**
● **The Ras Mohammed area.**
● **The Strait of Gubal.**

A - A dense colony of soft corals (Dendronephytha) extends its branches into the current, using the feathered tentacles in its polyps to grasp the plankton on which it feeds.

B - A crinoid with black feathered tentacles is attached to a large Porites coral formation. These constructor corals grow very slowly, about a centimeter a year, and it is estimated that the larger colonies are over a thousand years old.

C - Dense schools of jacks (Caranx sexfasciatus) patrol the surface waters, always on the lookout for prey. Their hunting technique is to dart into schools of fish in order to create confusion and isolate an individual fish, which becomes easy prey when separated from the school.

D - Hundreds of large barracudas gather during certain times of the year, drawn by the irresistible urge to reproduce.

THE STRAIT OF TIRAN

Located on the southern tip of the Gulf of Aqaba, the strait takes its name from the island of Tiran. About 4 miles separate the island, which is owned by Saudi Arabia but controlled by Egypt, and the eastern coast of the Sinai, and in the middle of this channel there are four semi-emerged reefs which are nothing more than the peaks of several submerged mountains that rise to the surface.

Around the reefs the walls descend vertically from the surface, reaching a bathymetric depth of 60 meters, and then plunge down into the abyss. The strait is quite deep, from 200 to 800 meters, and when the underwater currents meet the mountain range they create a movement of water that carries an incredible amount of plankton to the four reefs.

The nourishment carried in and the constant currents have permitted the growth of dense alcyonarians and true gorgonian forests on the submerged walls. The vertical walls of the reefs of Tiran are some of the most colorful and lively in the area. The currents also carry large schools of pelagic fish to the reef, including barracudas and jacks, followed by their predators, sharks. Tiran is in fact the place where shark sightings are most common. The best way to explore these walls is certainly in a drift dive. Dives usually take place along the southeast sides of the reefs; the current runs north at high tide, and the sea is usually calm here. Sometimes weather conditions make it possible to explore the west side of the reefs, which has the same conformation.

LOCAL DIVES

All the dives along the coastline from White Knight to Temple, just a few minutes away from the two landing stages at Sharm el-Maya and Naama Bay, are known as "local." The features of the sea floor are more or less the same for nearly all the dives: the reef descends in a brief drop of 5-7 meters, then the wall slopes much more gently to a bathymetric depth of 25-30 meters, where it once again becomes vertical and appears to plunge into the blue depths. The plateau you explore contains coral pinnacles that rise up like towers from the sea floor, in some cases reaching heights of 8-10 meters. Attached to these formations are dense clusters of brilliantly colored alcyonarians and gorgonians of various types and sizes. At the edge of the drop-off you may see pelagic fish like tunas and sharks, but the main objective of dives in this area is certainly to examine the clusters of invertebrates, with all the microfauna that hides there, and the endless variety of reef fish. In particular, in the area north of Ras um Sid, there are unusually large coral structures, primarily umbrella formations. In some areas there are permanent mooring lines, while in others, because the coastline offers no shelter, drift dives are the only alternative.

E

F

G

E - Fish-eye lenses will give you an unbroken view of the entire bay of Sharm el-Maya. The beach below, which you can reach by an elevator, is for those who would rather relax than dive.

F - Enormous formations of brightly colored alcyonarians, surrounded by swarms of anthias (Pseudanthias squamipinnis), *grow on the sheer vertical wall.*

G - Moving along the reef, you can see the ever-present gorgonian sea fans (Subergorgia) that grow perpendicular to the walls in search of waters rich with nourishment.

11

THE RAS MOHAMMED AREA

The Ras Mohammed district extends from Ras Za'atar to the coral towers of Shark and Jolanda reefs. This area, which is extremely beautiful and of enormous naturalistic interest, is on the southernmost tip of the Sinai and is the first and only protected area in the entire Red Sea. The southernmost part of the Ras Mohammed peninsula is distinguished by two rocky spits separated by a deep bay known as Hidden Bay. While the eastern area is a high promontory about 60 meters above sea level, the western area is low, with a sandy island separated by a narrow channel. In the channel grow mangrove forests which scientists have studied for years, trying to explain why these trees are growing so far north of their usual biological limit. Thousands of migrating swans stop at this natural oasis every year. The geographical position of the Sinai Peninsula, and in particular of Ras Mohammed, wedged in between the Gulf of Aqaba and the Gulf of Suez, forces large masses of waters to mix together, following the rhythm of the currents. The result is that enormous quantities of plankton are carried into the area, creating perfect conditions for activating the first link in a food chain that begins with invertebrates and ends with oceanic predators. There are masses of alcyonarians along the walls of the reef, and the gorgonian fans are exceptionally large; this is where the biodiversity of the entire Red Sea reaches its full splendor. At some times of the year the urge to reproduce calls thousands of jacks, barracudas, batfish, and surgeonfish to these magical waters. These animals will form true living walls that undulate in the open sea, and swimming among them can be a indescribably thrilling experience. Rules of Ras Mohammed National Park, applicable from Tiran to Sha'ab Ali. The following are prohibited:
- gathering or damaging any part of the reef, living or dead;
- throwing any type of anchor or walking on the corals;
- feeding or disturbing the fish;
- fishing with any kind of equipment;
- wearing gloves during dives;
- littering of any kind either on land or in the sea;
- driving motor vehicles on the beach.

A

B

C

A - The high walls sheer to the sea on the southern side of the Sinai Peninsula are often broken by deep cracks that were once the beds of rivers flowing into the sea. Often the underwater scene is a continuation of what we see on the surface.

B - An encounter with a giant manta is always thrilling. The two large cephalic fins protruding from the sides of its head that it uses to bring planktonic organisms to its mouth have given this elegant, peaceful creature the undeserved name of "sea devil."

C - A gorgonian in the foreground provides a beautiful close-up. The silhouettes of boats moored to a shamandura stand out on the surface. The prohibition on using mobile anchors has preserved the upper area of the reef.

D - Beautiful shipwrecks from different periods, now artificial reefs thickly encrusted by every type of coral, can be explored in full day trips or brief cruises from Sharm el-Sheikh. A myriad of life forms surrounds the metallic structures, making a dive onto one of these wrecks an unforgettable experience.

THE STRAIT OF GUBAL

The strait is bounded to the east by the southern area of the Sinai Peninsula, and to the west by the islands of Shadwan and Gubal. The sea floor in this area is mostly flat and sandy, and the depth, except for a few hollows, almost never exceeds 40 meters. There are two distinct reefs in this area: Sha'ab Mahmud and Sha'ab Ali. The long Mahmud reef runs parallel to the Sinai coast for about 6 miles, and includes a shallow, sandy-

E - A gorgonian has attached to the metallic structures within the Shag Rock wreck. The ship, which lies in shallow waters, has been completely covered by corals of every type and shape, and can even be seen from the surface.

D

E

F

detrital lagoon open to the south. Near the opening, a group of mushroom coral formations edge the lagoon. The line of the reef provides only two passageways to enter the lagoon, Small Crack and, farther north, Big Crack, and its southernmost branch is marked by the Beacon Rock lighthouse. Not far off is Sha'ab Ali, another coral system with alternating shallow lagoons and extensive semi-emerged coral formations. The southern tip of the maze of reefs that constitutes Sha'ab Ali is an isolated coral formation with an elongated form on which there is a lighthouse. Its name, Shag Rock, comes from the cormorants that are frequent visitors at its emerged coral areas. These areas are quite popular with scuba divers, as they contain true treasures to explore, including the most famous shipwrecks of the Red Sea: the *Thistlegorm*, the *Dunraven* and the *Sarah H*. All these ships sank at depths accessible to recreational divers and can thus be explored by all divers fascinated by shipwrecks.

F - The holds of the wreck of the Thistlegorm *still contain the cargo that the English cargo ship, which was sunk during the war in 1941, was transporting to Allied troops stationed in North Africa. Trucks, jeeps, motorcycles and other materiel can still be clearly seen within the sunken ship.*

G - The beam of an electronic flashlight illuminates the golden mass of a swarm of glassfish (Parapriacanthus guentheri). By day glassfish usually gather inside caves and crevices, while at night they come out to hunt zooplankton along the reef.

A - Diving boats usually have an area reserved for photographers so they can work on their equipment away from unwanted sprays of water. During the break between one dive and another, photographers exchange advice and adventures: a diving cruise is also a way to expand knowledge and compare experiences.

B - Video fans can also film scenes full of color and movement. A good light is necessary to give the colors of the reef their natural brilliance. While filming, remember to stand on sandy areas only, not on the corals.

C - The floors of the Red Sea are certainly more popular with photographers than any other sea beds in the world. Their beauty and the variety of subjects to photograph, along with the clear water, make spectacular pictures possible.

D - It is easy to approach the marine fauna of Sharm el-Sheikh, and if you know the proper techniques you can even use a super wide-angle lens to obtain effective images, like this reverse shot of a group of batfish with a turtle in the foreground.

E - Large gorgonian fans rise up from the floor. Sometimes the addition of a human figure can be useful to highlight the size of fish and corals.

A

B

C

D

UNDERWATER PHOTOGRAPHY

The floor of the Red Sea is certainly the most popular place in the world for underwater photographers. Since 1950, when Hans Hass, a pioneer in underwater photography, took the first shots in "Allah's aquarium," thousands of scuba divers have tried to capture the explosive colors of this underwater paradise on film. And it would truly be a shame, after a trip to this extraordinary world, if scuba divers did not bring

E

home pictures that relived their thrilling experiences here. The number of people who have taken up scuba diving has increased at a rate that would have been unheard of just a few years ago. This is doubtless due to more flexible training systems which nevertheless do not neglect the comfort and safety of students, and the creation and growth of diving centers, which are becoming increasingly professional. In areas like Sharm el-Sheikh, every year hundreds of people attend excellent scuba diving courses, giving their vacations a new and entertaining twist. One of the most absorbing and rewarding activities for scuba divers is underwater photography. To start with, you can follow the advice of any self-styled expert, but it's certainly better to take a special course where you will learn basic techniques which will allow you to take good pictures from the very start. I advise you not to plunge in right away, buying complicated professional cameras, but to start with the ever-popular *Nikonos* equipped with a standard lens and a good electronic TTL flash. The *Nikonos* system consists of an amphibious camera and a series of interchangeable lenses ranging from 80 mm for close-ups to two medium-format 35 mm and 28 mm lenses, which are ideal for fish or small portions of the reef, to wide-angle lenses like the 20 and 15 mm, which provide ample frames without having to move too far away from the subject. You can then graduate to the *Nikonos RS-AF*, an amphibious reflex camera with automatic focus lenses and sophisticated automatic mechanisms. With lenses that range from a 13 mm super wide-angle to a 50 mm micro, it will meet all your photography needs. Another solution for underwater photographers is to use a normal camera in a sealed underwater case. The advantage of this system is that you will have all the electronic functions of the camera and a wide range of lenses at your disposal. Quite economic underwater cases are now available on the market, such as the polycarbonate case.

The exceptional clarity of the waters at Sharm el-Sheikh, where sunlight filters down to great depths, makes it possible to obtain beautiful pictures in mixed light, using the camera's exposure meter to balance environmental lighting with the camera flash. You will obtain brilliantly colored fish and corals in the foreground, contrasting with the deep blue of the marine background.

Film suitable for this type of photography includes emulsions from 64 to 100 ASA. Don't forget about macrophotography, as you can find an endless array of subjects among the corals and alcyonarians, including crabs and hawkfish. You can use 25 or 50

F

F - Whip corals look three-dimensional when photographed against the light. When you use this technique, you need to calculate the flash according to the diaphragm setting, which will necessarily be rather low.

G - Underwater cameras can be used for fish portraits. To avoid coming too close to your subjects, you should use long focal lenses like the 105 mm or the 200 mm.

H - A small clown anemonefish curiously approaches the photographer, yet remains protected among the tentacles of its sea anemone host.

G

H

ASA film for more saturated colors and greater definition.

The waters of the South Sinai hold countless subjects to photograph, including clown anemonefish, mantas, sharks, tiny gobies, shrimps and schools of thousands of fish. It is important to use the right lens for each shot. After each dive, wash all your photography equipment by emerging it in fresh water for a few minutes and, at least once a day, check and gently lubricate all the OR you can reach. At least once a year you should have the camera checked by a specialized laboratory in order to test all the functions you can't check yourself. You will find numerous shops at Sharm el-

Sheikh and Naama Bay where you can purchase all types of film and develop and frame your slides. You can also rent underwater cameras and flash equipment at these photo shops. Even when you're taking pictures, never forget to keep your position under control.

Everything you see underwater is alive and has its place in a fragile ecosystem in which humans have no part, so enter this magical world of silence with respect, and try not to disturb its fantastic inhabitants.

Others will want to enjoy and thrill to the same marvels you have seen, so: Take only photos, leave only bubbles!

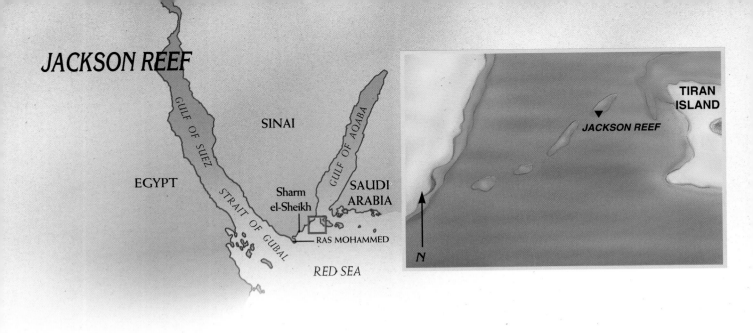

JACKSON REEF

EGYPT

SINAI

GULF OF SUEZ

STRAIT OF GUBAL

GULF OF AQABA

SAUDI ARABIA

Sharm el-Sheikh

RAS MOHAMMED

RED SEA

TIRAN ISLAND

JACKSON REEF

N

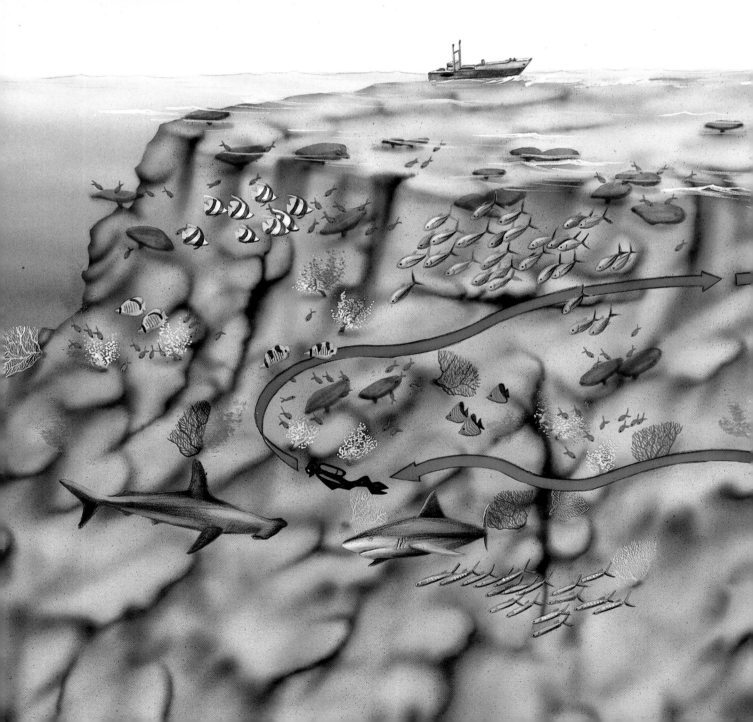

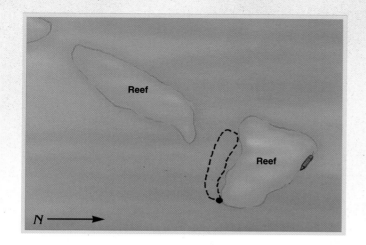

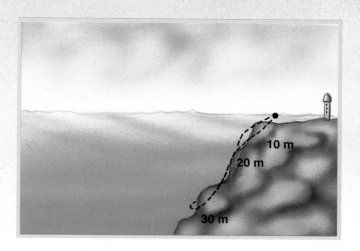

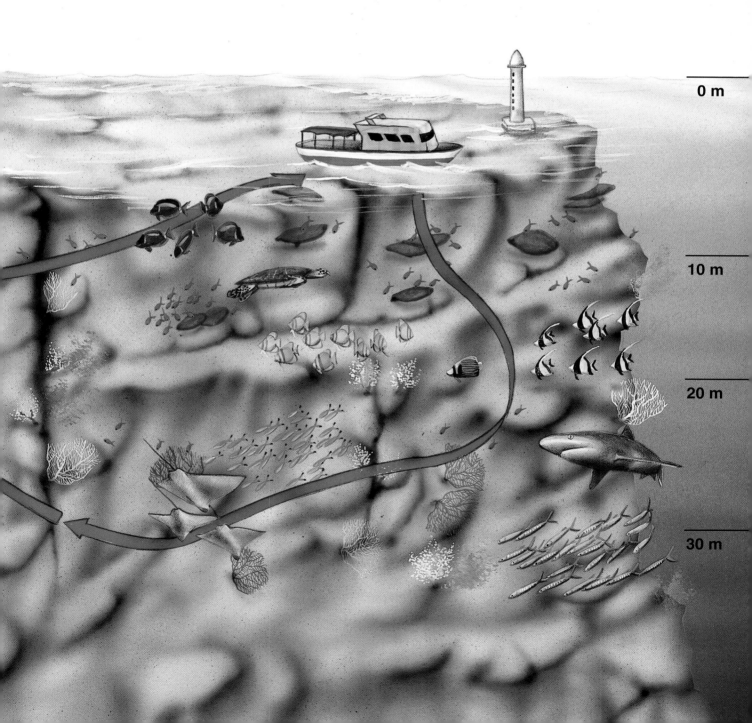

Jackson is the
northernmost of the
four semi-emerged reefs in
the Strait of Tiran.
The area is a little over an hour's
sail from Naama Bay, heading
north. The more or less circular
reef is marked to the east by
a red lighthouse and to the north
by the metallic remains of a
portion of the wreck of the *Lara*,
a Cypriot ship that sank on the
reef in 1985. Most of the ship,
which for years was perched
on the outer edge of the reef,
was removed to prevent it from

D

A

B

E

C

sinking and destroying part
of the coral reef. The metallic
structures underwater are already
well-encrusted with corals.
On the south side is a large
military mooring buoy.
There are two permanent
mooring lines on the south side,
which are reserved for diving
boats. Usually the divemaster
will reinforce the anchoring by
also tying the boat to a dead
coral on the surface.
Diving excursions usually start
from this area.

*B - The remains of the
Cypriot ship* Lara *are
visible on the northern
side of Jackson Reef.
The northwest sides
of this reef can only
be explored when the
sea is calm.*

*C - Silhouettes of boats
and divers stand out
against the light. The
walls of Jackson Reef
are richly decorated
with bushes of
alcyonarians and
plunge down
vertically to
unsounded depths.*

D - A solitary Arab angelfish (Pomacanthus maculosus) swims along the reef. This common species in the Red Sea is quite sociable and will curiously approach divers. It is easily identifiable by the showy yellow spots on its flanks.

E - A butterflyfish (Chaetodon fasciatus) moves among this dense coral formation in search of the coral polyps on which it feeds. This fish, which usually lives in pairs, may also gather in groups of about twenty individuals.

F - After female sea turtles reach maturity, they reproduce about every two years. They will deposit up to 150 eggs in holes they dig in the beach and then cover with sand. Incubation requires about two months, and the sex of the newborn turtles is determined by the temperature within the nest.

G - The currents rich with nourishment that sweep the reefs in this area encourage the luxuriant growth of soft corals. Alcyonarians in a variety of colors, from pink to violet, are growing above this protuberance.

H - In areas where the currents are periodically stronger, the gorgonian sea fans grow more densely and are larger and more robust than elsewhere. The largest fans may reach a width of three meters.

F

G

The wall of Jackson Reef, broken by numerous cracks, starting at the surface, descends vertically to a sandy plateau about 50 meters deep, which then plunges to the abyss.

Its constant exposure to currents has encouraged the growth of exceptionally large gorgonians and dense alcyonarians, and it is also an area where these currents make it possible to see all types of pelagic fish, including sharks. During the summer, on the sides most exposed to currents, it is not uncommon to see groups of hammerhead sharks patrolling the deeper waters. These meetings are quite frequent on the ridge that joins Jackson Reef to Woodhouse Reef at a depth of 30 meters.

H

The dive usually begins as you enter the water from the boat's stern platform, and swim on the surface until you reach the wall. Even during this first part of the dive, if you look down into the blue waters you will see dense schools of fusiliers followed by groups of jackfish and surgeonfish that crowd the upper layers of water.

When you approach the reef, begin your descent, keeping the wall to your right. You will immediately be impressed by the size and number of alcyonarians that cover the wall from the surface on down, with deep violet to red branches.

A - Pomacanthus imperator is considered the most beautiful of all tropical fish. This territorial angelfish is solitary, only joining others of its species during the reproductive season.

B - This photo clearly shows the dense branches that comprise the delicate structure of a gorgonian. Tiny fish and crustaceans live protected among its tangled branches.

C - A blue triggerfish (Pseudobalistes fuscus) patrols the reef in search of the sea urchins on which it feeds. The technique it uses to overcome the defenses of these echinoderms is to overturn them with a powerful jet of water to get to their vulnerable oral disk. This territorial species lives in sandy and detrital areas where it can dig holes for its eggs.

C

A

B

D

For seascapes, use a wide-angle lens. A fisheye lens is especially useful for framing the dense blooms of soft corals, perhaps by adding the silhouette of the boat against the light.
Continue the dive down to a depth of 25 meters, where you will see large sea fans and bushes of black coral similar to trees with drooping fronds.
If you look carefully among the branches, you will discover hawkfish and green damselfish. Being careful not to go too far

D - An elegant Pterois miles glides gracefully through the branches of a gorgonian. These members of the Scorpaenidae family, with pectoral fins similar to wings, are easy to approach, but divers should be careful not to disturb them, as they can inflict painful stings.

E - *Watching the elegant flight of an eagle ray* (Aetobatus narinari) *is certainly a thrilling part of any dive.*

F -
The unmistakable form of a hammerhead shark (Sphyraena lewini) *materializes as if out of nowhere. Usually larger individuals leave the school and live a solitary existence.*

forward, where you will be carried away by the current far from the place where the boat is moored, come to the point where you can see sharks swimming by in the blue depths.
For good photos of these lords of the sea, use a 28 mm lens mounted on a manageable amphibious camera.
Return to your starting point and explore the reef at depths of 10 to 15 meters, where you may see turtles and groupers hidden among the crevices.

H

E

I

F

G

The upper part of the reef is extraordinary in its colors and life forms. A carpet of yellow and pink alcyonarians has colonized the wall, and the reef inhabitants swim all about: butterflyfish, parrotfish, and surgeonfish with colors made even more brilliant by the bright sunlight.
In some areas you will see cavities with sandy floors a few meters from the surface, inhabited by swarms of emperors and pipefish. This is an ideal area for photographing fish in their own habitat using standard 50 or 60 mm lenses.
If you are experienced enough, you can use drift dive techniques to explore the eastern side of Jackson, where you may see gray sharks.

G - *The waters opposite the reefs of Tiran are one of the points where sharks are most often sighted. A gray shark* (Carcharhinus amblyrhynchos) *veers sharply away from the group of divers who had curiously approached it.*

H - *Fusiliers* (Caesio suevica) *swim tirelessly in their frenetic search for zooplankton. These fish, which can reach 30 centimeters in length, always move in large schools to avoid attacks by large predators.*

I - *A group of jacks curiously approaches two divers. The floors of Sharm el-Sheikh are considered some of the best places in the world to photograph fish.*

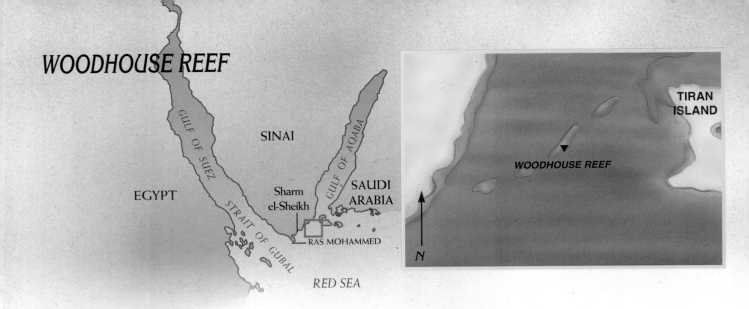

WOODHOUSE REEF

GULF OF SUEZ

SINAI

EGYPT

GULF OF AQABA

STRAIT OF GUBAL

Sharm el-Sheikh

SAUDI ARABIA

RAS MOHAMMED

RED SEA

TIRAN ISLAND

WOODHOUSE REEF

N

0 m

10 m

20 m

30 m

40 m

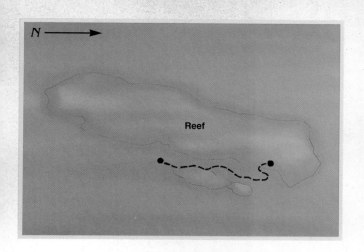

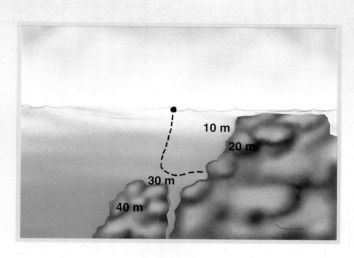

A

A - Red encrusting sponges colonize areas the hard corals have not overtaken, and sometimes even cover the bases of the trunks of alcyonarians. Sponges are filtering organisms which grow on the reef in various forms and colors.

B - The enormous fans of the gigantic gorgonians in the Red Sea (Subergorgia hicksoni) have pointed spicules along their surfaces that effectively protect them from parasites and predators.

C - The alcyonarians on the northern side of Woodhouse Reef reach record dimensions, and their extended polyps filter the water for precious nourishment. Gobies and expertly camouflaged crustaceans take shelter among their arborescent structures.

D - A group of anthias (Pseudanthias squamipinnis) moves jerkily above an imposing formation of hard corals. Young members of this species have different colors depending on their sex: females are yellow-orange with a narrow violet band near their eyes, while males are fuchsia with a red spot on the pectoral fin.

E - Groups of various fish swim near the cracks in the walls. If you approach them too quickly, they will take refuge in their lairs, only to reappear curiously after a few moments.

B

Woodhouse is the second reef in the Strait of Tiran, coming from the north. It is elongated in form and located between Jackson and Thomas reefs, and is about one hour from Naama Bay.
This is certainly the least popular of the four reefs located between the eastern coast of the Sinai and the island of Tiran.
This is not because this reef offers fewer attractions, but because the dive here is difficult. There are no permanent mooring lines along Woodhouse Reef, so drift dives are necessary. The elongated shape of the reef offers no shelter to boats, so your

C

return on board may be complicated by waves and currents. You should dive only if you are experienced and when weather conditions are perfect. Normally dives take place along the eastern side, where the wall descends vertically to a depth of 30 meters. At the north end, at a depth of 35 meters, a second coral wall runs parallel to the main reef, but the canyon created between the two is too deep to visit.
A little farther north of the deep gorge, at a depth of 15 meters, the walls widens into a sandy terrace scattered with small coral mushrooms.
The constant currents, which

D

F

bring in nourishment, have encouraged the growth of gorgonians, with their fans floating at right angles to the wall. At a depth of 20 to 30 meters, there are luxuriant reddish-brown bushes of black coral, and near the reef is an incredible variety of fish. Turtles are commonly seen resting on the corals as they break off pieces of the sponges on which they feed.
Despite the extraordinary sights on the wall, you should always take a look out to the open sea, where you can see groups of eagle rays "flying" elegantly in the current, and an occasional whitetip shark.

E

G

F - Spectacularly-shaped, vividly-colored gorgonians grow on the walls. These members of the subclass Octocorallia *have a horny skeleton which is usually covered with a softer sheath. The distribution of gorgonians depends on the currents.*

*G - Dense groups of bigeye trevallies (*Caranx sexfasciatus)*, like these darting past the photographer, gather in areas swept by currents.*

*H - A great number of fish. Here one can see some orange anthias (*Pseudanthias squamipinnis) *take shelter close to the coral formations that richly grow along the barrier reef.*

I - The vertical walls of the barrier reef offer vast surface areas to the flow of currents carrying nutrients to the coral polyps and consequently facilitate the growth of a great number of marine life forms.

H

I

25

A - The wall of Woodhouse Reef is often broken by sandy terraces with large, rounded corals.

B - This photograph shows the variety of colors possible for alcyonarians. The sun illuminates and brightens this small wall, which is a true coral jewel.

C - A butterflyfish (Heniochùs intermedius) swims near a formation of Tubastrea. These fish live in pairs, often sheltered by plate coral formations around which they stake out their territories. They feed on zooplankton, but also on invertebrates they find on the sea floor.

C

A

B

D

D - During the day, the leopard shark (Stegostoma fasciatum) rests lazily on the sandy areas of the reef. Timid and very difficult to approach, it is primarily nocturnal and comes out after sunset to search among the corals for the crustaceans, sea snakes and small fish on which it feeds. The surface of its mantle is traversed by longitudinal ribbing, and its tail alone is almost as long as its entire body. The black spots on its brown-yellow body give it its name.

E - An encounter with a great silvery school of barracudas is certainly an exciting experience for any diver.

There are also large swarms of fusiliers, into which big jackfish sometimes make rapid incursions.

Along the sandy areas, it is not uncommon to see a leopard shark lying lazily on the bottom. This dive begins about 150 meters south of the northern tip of Woodhouse Reef. After going down to about 27 meters deep, keep the wall to your left and move forward toward the canyon. Once you have reached this deep crack, ascend diagonally to the sandy platform. This is usually the point where your ascent to decompression depth begins. When the sea is calm and the current is weak, you can try to reach the northern point of the reef and go around it until you reach the western side. The wall is full of crevices richly adorned with soft corals, and near the surface there are large, solitary barracudas.

End your dive by surfacing near the reef, and swim to the boat from the surface.

It is difficult to recommend a lens for this dive, because there are so many subjects that any lens could work.

You could use 15 to 20 mm lenses for seascapes with gorgonian sea fans and black corals, while 28 to 35 mm lenses are better for picking out subjects like eagle rays or sharks against the deep blue of the sea.

E

F

G

F - Eagle rays (Aetobatus narinari) are some of the most fascinating creatures in the marine world. They may have a wingspan of over two meters and be over two and a half meters long.

G - An encounter with a whitetip reef shark (Triaenodon obesus) always makes less expert divers feel apprehensive, but this rather shy creature, which feeds on parrotfish and other small crustaceans, is certainly no threat to divers.

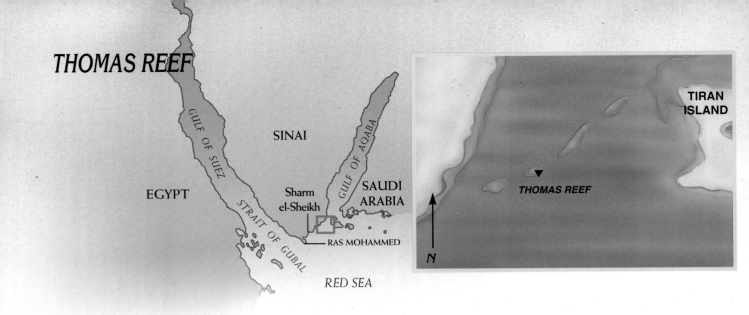

THOMAS REEF

GULF OF SUEZ

SINAI

GULF OF AQABA

EGYPT

STRAIT OF GUBAL

Sharm
el-Sheikh

SAUDI
ARABIA

RAS MOHAMMED

RED SEA

TIRAN
ISLAND

THOMAS REEF

N

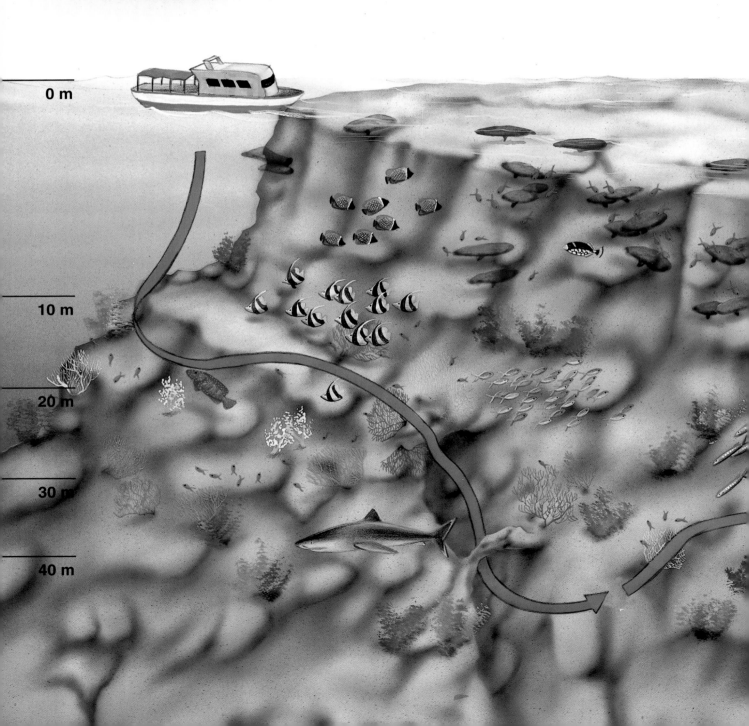

0 m

10 m

20 m

30 m

40 m

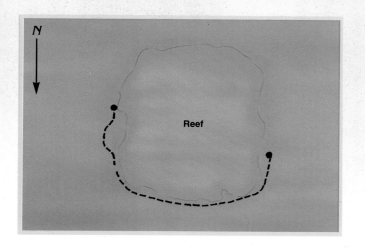

Reef

N

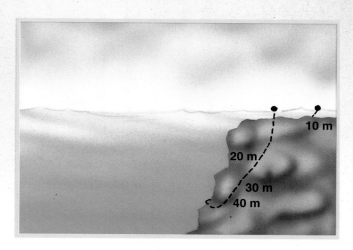

10 m

20 m

30 m

40 m

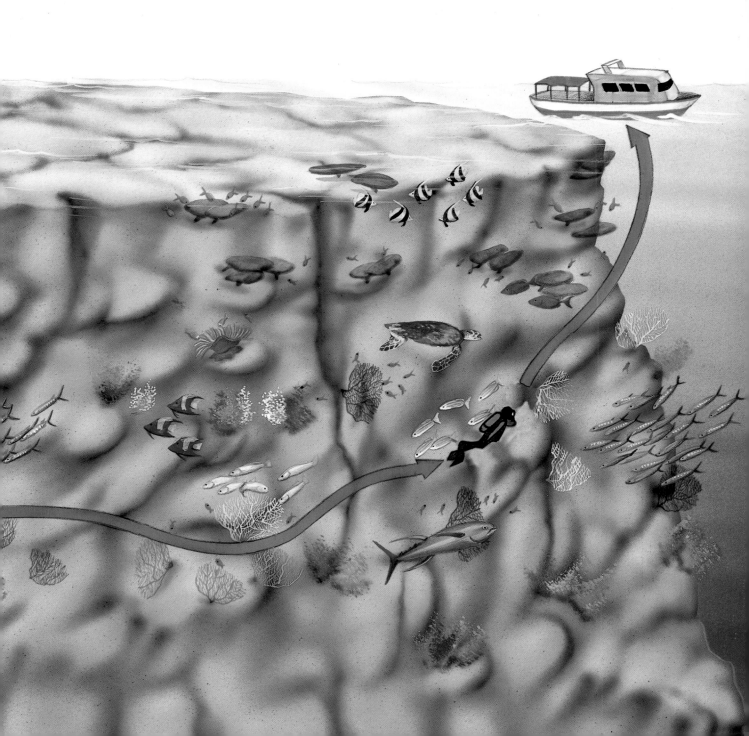

Thomas is the smallest of the four reefs of Tiran, and is located between Woodhouse and Gordon. Given its size and circular shape, it is possible to explore it completely in just one dive. The diving area is about a one hour sail from Naama Bay. There is a permanent mooring line on the southeast side of the plateau, but most people prefer to explore Thomas Reef in a drift dive. The boat's poop deck should be just a few meters from the reef, and you'll dive into the water and immediately begin your descent. The shallower part contains endless umbrella coral formations, beneath which are

A

B

C

D

A, B - Thomas Reef's treasure is its alcyonarians, which are extraordinarily concentrated on the walls of this reef. When the corals are turgid with their polyps extended, they offer a truly unique spectacle for divers.

C - A silvery cascade of glassfish (Parapriacanthus guentheri) arrives from above to embellish this part of the reef with its reflections. Delicate red alcyonarians grow on the walls.

groupers lying in wait in the shadows, and the whole range of tropical fish swims around luxuriant, pale pastel alcyonarians. Quite often during this first part of the dive, you'll see turtles which can be easily approached and which sometimes follow divers for quite some time. If this happens to you, don't try to touch these shy animals, as you would only frighten them unnecessarily and drive them out of the area permanently. Keep the wall to your left and head north, reaching a sandy plateau at a depth of 20-25 meters, interrupted by low coral mushrooms. This fairly large terrace ends at the drop-off to your right that plunges into the abyss. One of the attractions of the area is the enormous gorgonian that grows on the sea floor; it is more than two meters tall with a linear development of 7-8 meters, and is a popular subject for underwater photographers, who often add a human figure to their photos to give an idea of the size of the sea fans. Brightly colored emperor angelfish swim around the gorgonian, and if you explore among the delicate lacework you will find pipefish, tiny crabs and skillfully camouflaged gobies that are the joy of macrophotography fans. When the moon is full, titan triggerfish deposit their eggs in this area. They are particularly aggressive to anyone who approaches their nests, so if you don't want to get bitten, stay away from triggerfish when you see them near these sandy depressions. When you reach the end of the plateau, the reef breaks off from the main wall, forming a deep, narrow canyon that plunges down to great depths. This is the famous Thomas Canyon. The canyon is too deep for recreational diving, but it is still extremely interesting to examine this fracture in the reef and its arches. Pelagic fish such as large tunas and gray sharks are common in this area. As you start your ascent, you'll approach the wall again, passing thick bushes of black coral, with branches covered with thousands of polyps that filter nourishment carried in by the water. At a certain point, you'll feel

the gentle current that carried you change direction; you've come to the north side of the reef, where you need to ascend to make your safety decompression stop.
As you decompress at a depth of 4-5 meters, you'll be able to see small cavities and crevices where reef inhabitants frenetically carry on their everyday life. Once you reach the surface, you'll find the boat waiting for you not far off. This area can be photographed with wide-angle lenses, but if you have an underwater camera and a 28-70 mm zoom you can take different kinds of photos without losing once in a lifetime shots.

F

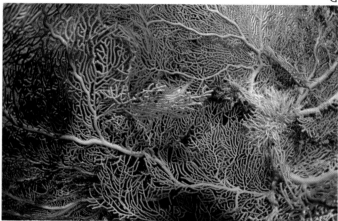

G

E

H

*F - Sea turtles have swum tirelessly in all the oceans of the world for thousands of years. These incredible reptiles have changed very little since their first appearance on the planet, and man is the only threat to their survival.
A diver approaches a peaceful* Eretmochelys imbricata, *perhaps the most beautiful and elegant of the sea turtles.*

G - The rigid structures of the gorgonian sea fans provide a support for other types of corals as well. In this case, a white coral (Seriatopora hystrix) *has colonized a large branch.
A hawkfish* (Oxycirrhites typus) *camouflaged among its branches lies in wait to attack small fish.*

H - A rare formation of whip corals is so flexible that the current can bend it almost in half without damaging it.

D - The red bodies of anthias adorn a dense formation of black coral (Antipathes). *The great bushes of black coral on the sea floors of Sharm el-Sheikh are in excellent health, unlike those in other parts of the world, where they have almost disappeared due to indiscriminate gathering.*

E - Two large grunts (Diagramma pictum) *rest sheltered by a large formation of* Acropora *umbrella corals. Grunts usually gather in small groups near the sandy floors where they find the invertebrates on which they feed.*

GORDON REEF

GULF OF SUEZ

GULF OF AQABA

SINAI

EGYPT

SAUDI ARABIA

Sharm el-Sheikh

STRAIT OF GUBAL

RAS MOHAMMED

RED SEA

TIRAN ISLAND

GORDON REEF

N

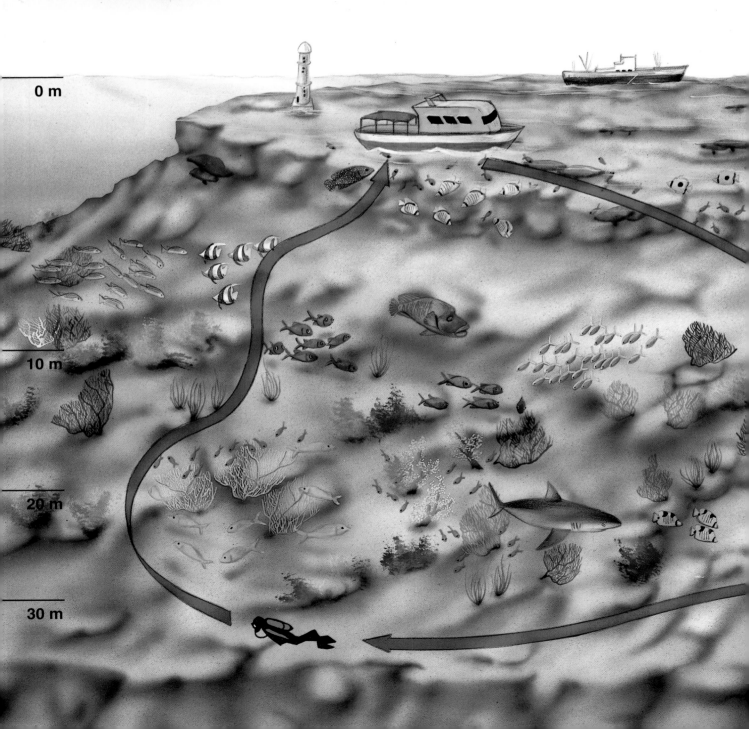

0 m

10 m

20 m

30 m

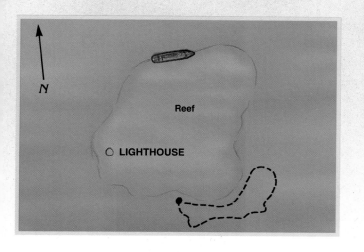

ordon is the southernmost of the four reefs of Tiran. It is nearly circular in form and is unmistakable due to the wreck of the cargo ship *Loullia*, which collided with the reef in 1981, remaining trapped in upright position on the emerged part of the reef. The area is less than one hour from Naama Bay. The upper reef is interesting for snorkelers as well, and sea anemones and their clown anemone fish, butterflyfish and red groupers are only a few of the creatures you can see from the surface. Dives at Gordon Reef are not particulary difficult and are suitable for every diver. Moor the boat on the south side, well sheltered from the waves, near a wide plateau that runs from 10 to 20 meters deep. Begin the dive by crossing the coral foundation diagonally to the north, until you reach a depth of about 25 meters. During this first part of the dive you'll pass several coral formations scattered on the plateau; around them are various types of parrotfish intent on breaking off the coral with their strong beaks. Motionless at the water's surface, trumpetfish with their long, cylindrical bodies the same color as the water are nearly invisible as they wait for prey which they will suck into their long mouths. The reef is at its best at a depth of 25 meters, with large sea fans that reach heights and widths of over 2 meters, undulating in the gentle current in search of food. Colored

C

A

B

D

A - In this view one can observe Gordon Reef and the wreck of the Loullia.

B - Groups of yellow goatfish (Parupenus cyclostomus) *patrol the coral floors, using their long barbels to flush out the small fish on which they feed.*

C - Diving boats moor on the shamandura *set into the south wall of Gordon Reef. From this point, depending on the current, you can dive in various directions.*

D - When using a closed circuit breathing apparatus (Rebreather), which creates no bubbles and thus no noise, you can approach fish without frightening them and take photographs which would otherwise be difficult to obtain.

E - A coral grouper (Cephalopholis miniata) curiously approaches the photographer's lens. These members of the Serranidae family, which are a constant presence during dives in the Red Sea, live in small groups, where the male is the largest individual.

F - This butterflyfish (Chaetodon semilarvatus) lives only in the Red Sea. Its lemon yellow color and the black spot near the eye make it unmistakable.

G - The multi-colored body of an emperor angelfish (Pomacanthus imperator) adds to the extraordinary explosion of colors on this coral plateau.

H - Eagle rays gliding elegantly in the blue depths are most common around midday. In the late afternoon these creatures go to shallow detrital sea beds to feed, where they use their mouths, which can be extended like a proboscis, to suck up worms and crustaceans from the sea floor.

I - Moving slowly, the photographer has come so close to this shark (Triaenodon obesus) that he can take a close-up shot. Whitetip sharks are creatures of habit who are rather territorial: during the day they lie on sandy clearings or take refuge in narrow cracks in the reef, while more rarely they can be seen swimming in the open water.

alcyonarians are often attached to their bases. Bands of yellow goatfish scour every protuberance of the floor with their barbels, in search of the small fish on which they feed. Yellow jacks can often be seen among the goatfish; they use the group to camouflage themselves and approach their prey without being seen. Various types of colorful soft corals form an almost unbroken carpet that offers refuge to small crabs and brightly colored shrimp. Out to sea, you may spot whitetip sharks passing by, and when the current is right, groups of eagle rays as well. On your return, you'll see several metal barrels, perhaps the remains of a shipwreck. At about 15 meters deep you'll see

a sandy depression known as "Amphitheater" or "Shark Swimming Pool", where in the early morning you are likely to see whitetip sharks resting after a night hunting. Come back under the boat and spend your last few minutes at a depth of 5 ` meters, often in the company of a large humphead wrasse. When the sea is calm during the high tide, with the current running north, you can do a drift dive from the mooring line and emerge at the north end of the reef. At low tide, you can begin the dive near the wreck and, heading south, explore the west side, ending your dive under the lighthouse. In this case your should explore the inside of the cracks on the upper reef, where whitetip sharks often live.

F

G

H

I

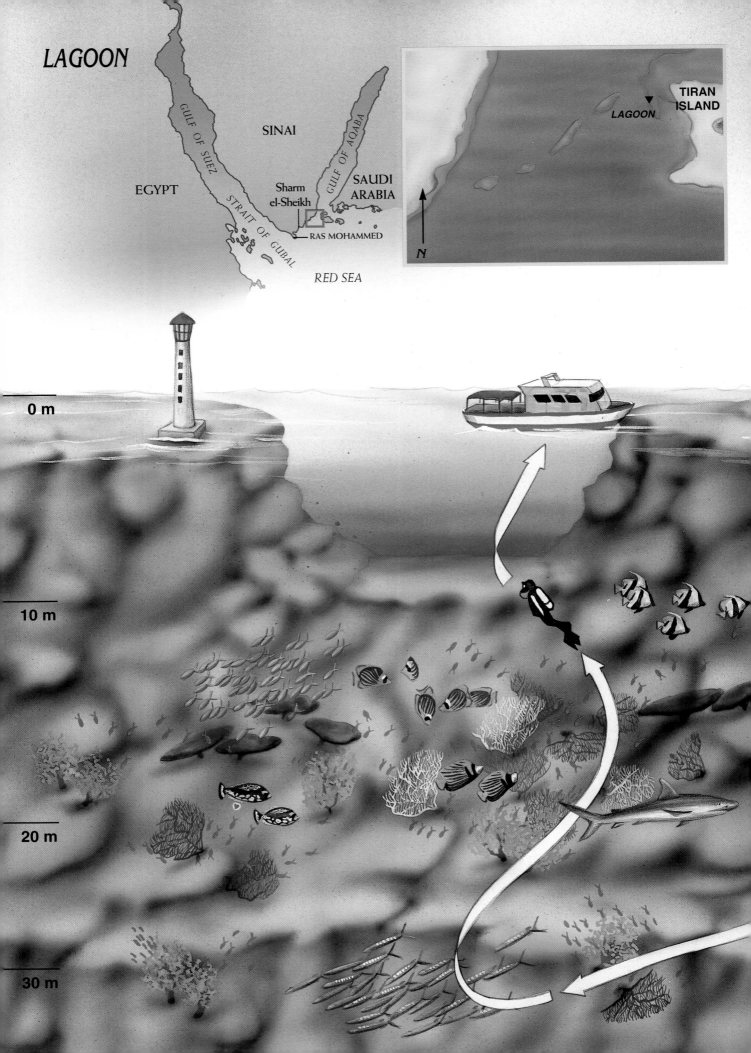

LAGOON

GULF OF SUEZ

SINAI

GULF OF AQABA

EGYPT

STRAIT OF GUBAL

Sharm
el-Sheikh

SAUDI
ARABIA

RAS MOHAMMED

RED SEA

TIRAN
ISLAND

LAGOON

N

0 m

10 m

20 m

30 m

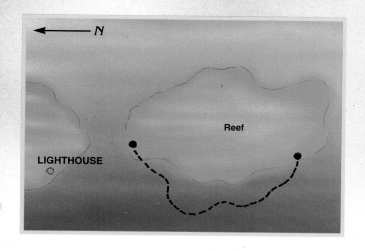

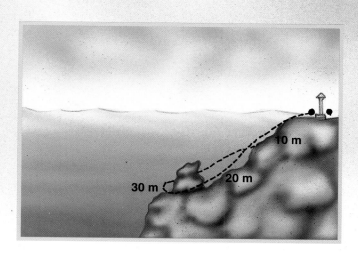

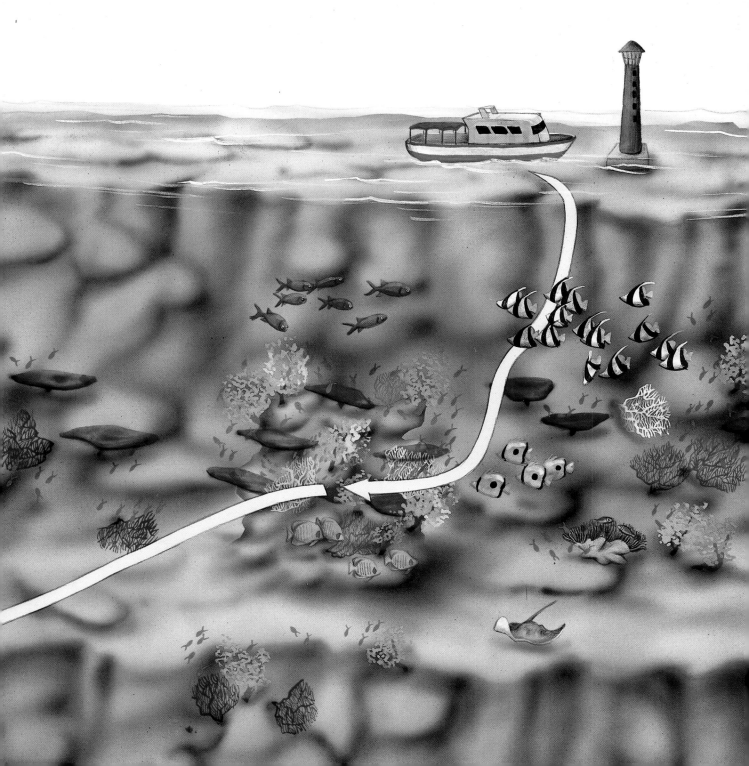

Lagoon is on the island of Tiran, an hour and a half north of Naama Bay. The waters around the island, which gives its name to the strait as well, are almost entirely closed to diving. Of the few areas open to divers, Lagoon is certainly the most interesting.

As soon as you leave the deep inlet of Naama, you will see the mountainous profile of the island of Tiran, whose buttresses continue as steep walls under the sea. At more or less the same height as semi-emerged Jackson Reef, this reef, which runs out from the island's coastline, forms a beautiful azure lagoon about 10 meters deep that is so

C

A

B

D

blue it looks like a swimming pool. The lagoon can be entered from a narrow pass, and when weather conditions are not optimal, the daily boats moor in these calm waters for lunch after a dive around one of the four reefs in the Strait of Tiran. There are several mooring lines within the lagoon.

The emerged portions of the reef are indicated by two lighthouses: a white and red one farther north and a green one to the far south. The walls of the lagoon facing the open sea are rather steep, and there is no place to anchor your boat, making a drift dive the only alternative. Dive in from the boat near the shallow waters a little

north of the green lighthouse. The current, which is usually quite weak, runs north and will carry divers to the end of the dive near one of the passes entering the lagoon.

The regular movements of the water carry in large quantities of microorganisms to this area, thus encouraging the growth of enormous gorgonians and luxuriant bushes of soft corals. Even at 10 meters deep there are large sea fans which sometimes grow so close to each other that they form a sort of forest. Within the tangle of branches the little inhabitants of these delicate formations teem frenetically: small gobies that become almost invisible due to their semi-transparent bodies, thin pipefish that move sinuously in search of the tiny crustaceans on which they feed, hawkfish with long pointed snouts, resting perfectly motionless and ready to dart out and snatch any small fish who unwisely comes too close. All divers should learn to examine the reef for its smaller inhabitants, as they have just as strange forms and colors as their larger counterparts. During your underwater itinerary, you'll pass pinnacle-shaped coral clusters. These more or less cylindrical formations, which rise several meters from the sea bed, host colonies of colorful anthias and splendid cascades of purple alcyonarians, while in the more sheltered areas there are pairs of masked butterflyfish.

Forms of life on these blocks of coral also include large anemones with their ever-present clown anemonefish. Blue-spotted stingrays are common in the sandy areas, where they usually remain motionless, partially buried in the sand, ready to flee if you come too close.

The relative proximity of the emerging reefs of Tiran, around which are numerous pelagic fish, makes it likely that you may spot a small whitetip shark during this dive as it scours the crevices of the reef.

At about 20 meters deep, the incessant work of the coral polyps has constructed umbrella-shaped coral structures with delicate branches. When you gaze at these spectacular structures, which may reach up to 2 meters in diameter, you should be very careful to keep your position neutral to avoid destroying dozens of years of nature's work with a careless blow from your flipper.

Excellent seascapes can be shot during this dive using a wide-angle lens. For those who prefer close-up photos, I recommend using an underwater camera and 105 mm lens, so you can remain at some distance from your subjects and take photographs without disturbing them.

E

A - Gorgonians are a constant presence along the outer wall of Lagoon. There are often intricate formations of red sponges (Clathria reinwardti) at the base of the fans, making a colorful subject for a photo.

B - A turkeyfish swims around a gorgonian. These members of the Scorpaenidae family often live near gorgonians, which provide excellent hunting grounds due to the myriad of fish that live within their tangled branches.

C - Alcyonarians, with their infinite shades of color and their bizarre forms, are certainly one of the most popular photographic subjects on the reef.

D - A clown anemonefish (Amphiprion bicinctus) rests safely among the tentacles of a sea anemone. These extremely territorial fish spend their entire lives associated with the same anemone.

E - This tiny goby (Bryaninops youngei) reaches no more than three centimeters in size and lives exclusively on whip corals (Cirripathes anguinea). It moves quickly along the entire length of its host, usually in pairs.

F - A solitary butterflyfish (Chaetodon semilarvatus) swims near a formation of fire coral (Millepora dichotoma).

G - When you photograph alcyonarians be careful to set your camera flash carefully, because their translucent structures absorb and reflect a great deal of light.

H - A jackfish (Carangoides bajad) can often be spotted among the yellow goatfish (Parupenus cyclostomus), where, using the cover of the group, it changes color to match the fish around it, thus enabling it to pass unnoticed as it approaches its prey, which it attacks with lightning-quick darts.

I - This rare example of an emperor shrimp (Periclemenes imperator) finds shelter among the bumps on the mantle of a sea cucumber.

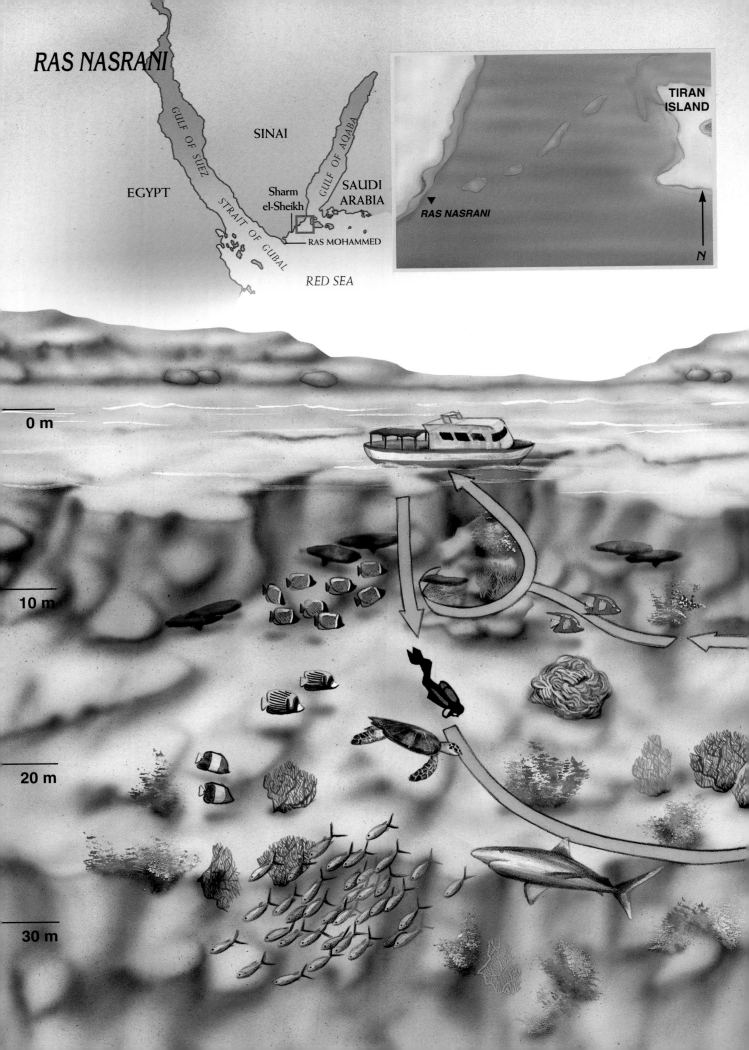

RAS NASRANI

GULF OF SUEZ
SINAI
GULF OF AQABA
EGYPT
Sharm el-Sheikh
SAUDI ARABIA
STRAIT OF GUBAL
RAS MOHAMMED
RED SEA

TIRAN ISLAND
RAS NASRANI
N

0 m
10 m
20 m
30 m

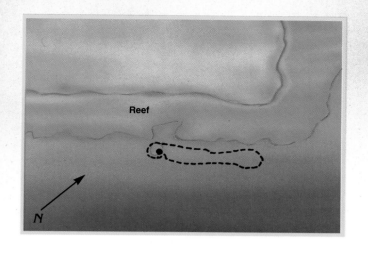

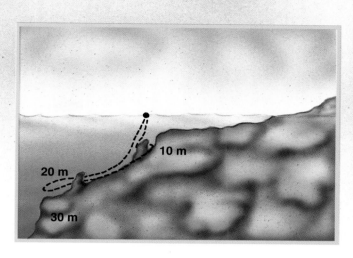

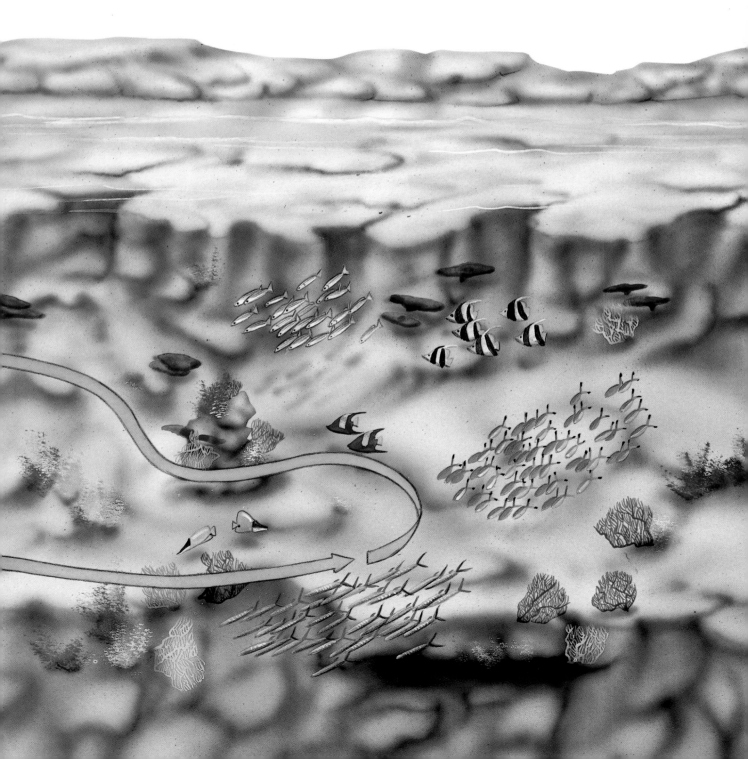

A - The barrier reef
is most luxuriant
toward the open
sea, where the
currents bring in
nourishment to the
coral polyps.
A small lagoon
forms between the
reef and the coast,
accumulating
skeletons of dead
corals which then
transform into
white coral sand.

B - Silvery jacks
gleam with a
metallic shine
in the light of the
camera flash. When
photographing
these fish, it is
important to
consider the high
reflecting power
of their skin.

C - This small
hawkfish
(Oxycirrhites typus)
seems perched
among the
branches of a tree.
Hawkfish are
hermaphrodites
and live in harems:
when the male
dies, the dominant
female changes sex.

A

B

C

D

Ras Nasrani, one of the most spectacular diving areas in the Strait of Tiran, is a little less than an hour's sail north of Naama Bay. Almost all divers who arrive at Sharm el-Sheikh have seen this area, at least from above: Tas Nasrani is just a few hundred meters from the international airport.
The diving area is located south of the cape of Nasrani, sheltered from the northerly winds. Here as well, there are two permanent mooring lines where you can anchor your boat. From the surface, the wall of the reef drops to a depth of 4-6 meters, forming several small inlets with caves inhabited by swarms of glassfish. This part of the reef can be quite interesting for snorkelers, too. Several coral formations rise from the shallow bottom and offer support for small brown gorgonians and soft corals that look vaguely like broccoli, while red coral groupers peep out curiously from their lairs.
One of these masses is completely surrounded by a cloud of tiny glassfish pursued by their primary predator: the redmouth grouper. This shallower area contains a magnificent coral garden, illuminated in all its beauty by the sun. The coral platform then descends in a gentle slope to a depth of 25-30 meters, transforming into a vertical wall that plunges into the deep blue depths. This is the reign of pelagic fish, and you may see tunas, jackfish and sometimes a few whitetip sharks come to the edge of the drop-off, where they can be photographed at close range. At a bathymetric depth of between 15 and 30 meters, there are magnificent gorgonians surrounded by butterflyfish. Some of the fans grow so close to each other that they create inextricable bushes, and if you explore among the delicate lacework you will see small hawkfish lying in wait for their prey. Luxuriant, brightly colored soft corals grow everywhere, with skillfully camouflaged, tiny gobies on their stems. This is the most interesting part of the wall, with a multitude of

D - The views from within the caves in the shallower areas of the Ras Nasrani reef are extremely beautiful. Be careful not to raise suspended particles as you enter these caves. Large **Plectropomus** groupers, who are quite easy to approach, lie in wait in the darker recesses of these caverns.

E - A diver approaches a bush of alcyonarians, with the life of the reef teeming all around it. This is another example of the wealth of underwater life in this sea.

F - A diver approaches a gorgonian as a turkeyfish (Pterois miles) circles it in its constant search for food.

G

I

E

H

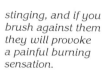

F

G - These corals are just as fragile as they are beautiful. All it takes is an accidental blow of your fins to destroy years of work by their constructor polyps.

H - Red encrusting sponges have colonized the dead portion of a colony of fire corals (Millepora dichotoma). The polyps of fire corals are quite stinging, and if you brush against them they will provoke a painful burning sensation.

I - This species of hard coral (Turbinaria mesenterina) has luminous yellow vertical laminae similar to crumpled leaves. Groups of Turbinaria can cover areas several square meters in size.

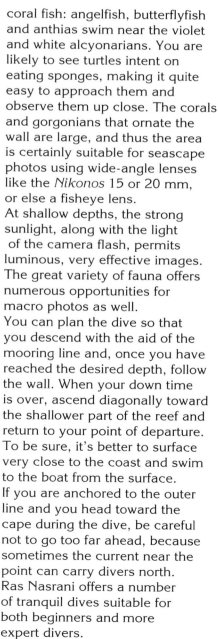

coral fish: angelfish, butterflyfish and anthias swim near the violet and white alcyonarians. You are likely to see turtles intent on eating sponges, making it quite easy to approach them and observe them up close. The corals and gorgonians that ornate the wall are large, and thus the area is certainly suitable for seascape photos using wide-angle lenses like the *Nikonos* 15 or 20 mm, or else a fisheye lens.

At shallow depths, the strong sunlight, along with the light of the camera flash, permits luminous, very effective images. The great variety of fauna offers numerous opportunities for macro photos as well.

You can plan the dive so that you descend with the aid of the mooring line and, once you have reached the desired depth, follow the wall. When your down time is over, ascend diagonally toward the shallower part of the reef and return to your point of departure. To be sure, it's better to surface very close to the coast and swim to the boat from the surface.

If you are anchored to the outer line and you head toward the cape during the dive, be careful not to go too far ahead, because sometimes the current near the point can carry divers north.

Ras Nasrani offers a number of tranquil dives suitable for both beginners and more expert divers.

WHITE KNIGHT

EGYPT

SINAI

SAUDI ARABIA

GULF OF SUEZ

GULF OF AQABA

STRAIT OF GUBAL

Sharm el-Sheikh

RAS MOHAMMED

RED SEA

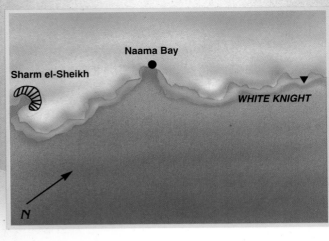

Sharm el-Sheikh

Naama Bay

WHITE KNIGHT

N

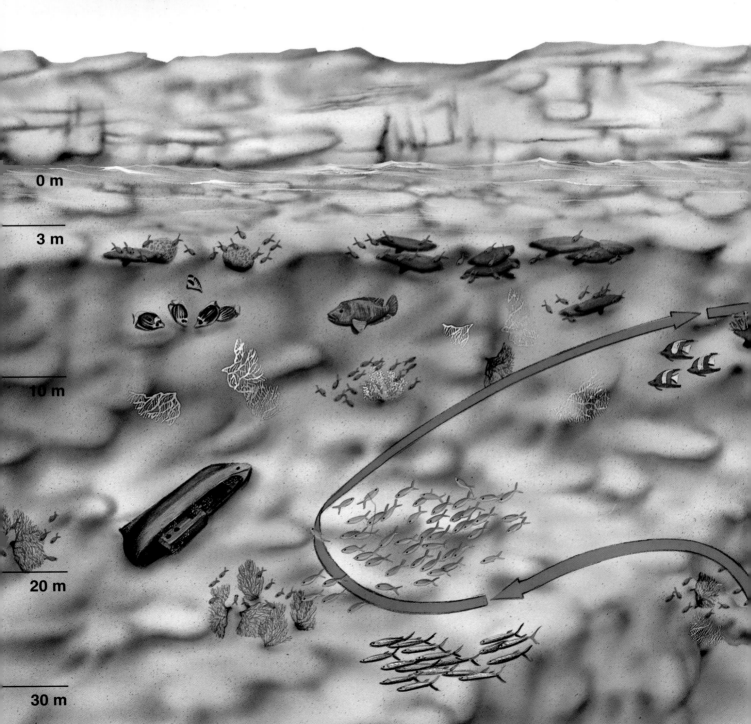

0 m

3 m

10 m

20 m

30 m

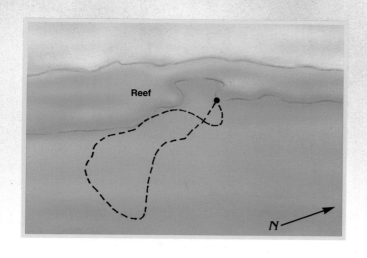

Reef

N

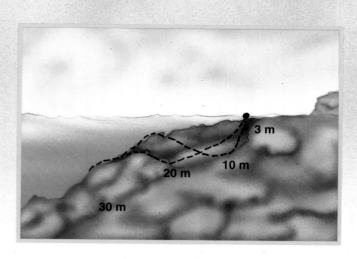

3 m

10 m

20 m

30 m

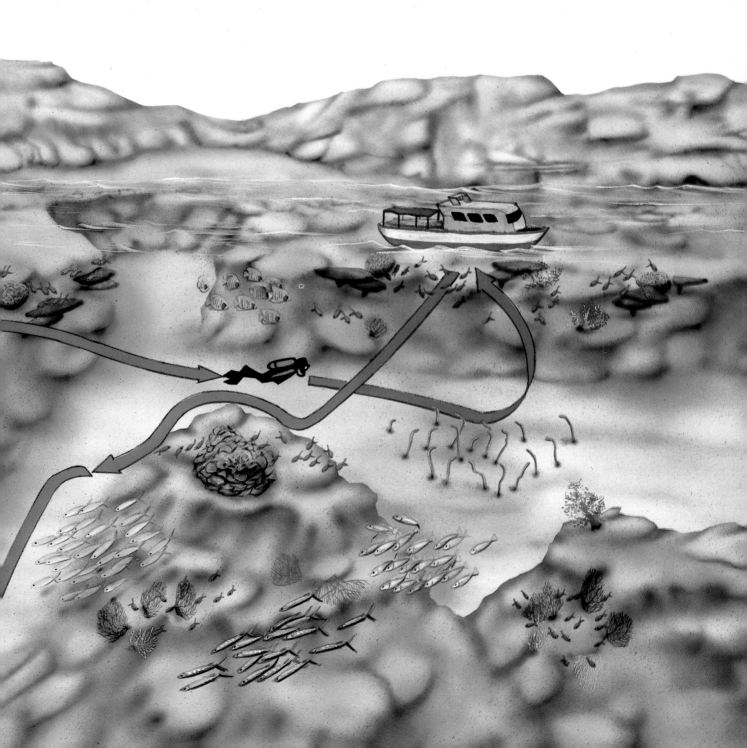

White Knight is a small bay north of the gulf of Shark's Bay. It is about a forty minute sail from the Naama Bay pier. A mooring line is set into the center of the floor of the inlet. It is long enough to reach the surface, and the boat can thus be easily anchored a short distance from the reef. This area is especially full of attractions, including for snorkelers, who will find many sights to admire in the upper areas of the reef. The coast is rather shallow, and a small beach breaks the line of the reef. This is an excellent place to try out your scuba equipment for the first time and is a good location for your first forays into the open water during

C

A- The brilliant color of this Turbinaria makes a very popular subject for underwater photographers. Small, camouflaged crustaceans can be seen among its whorls. Most of its polyps are on the outer edges, and their tentacles are expanded throughout the day. Turbinaria's complex form is due the coral colony's need to give the algae that keep it alive as much surface area as possible.

B - As you leave the White Knight canyon, you will pass dense groups of fish, including yellow goatfish.

C - Turgid alcyonarians grow on a gorgonian sea fan, forming a brightly colored composition.

D - These coral formations, which are quite common in the shallow waters of the Red Sea, are home to astounding worlds of animal and plant life.

A

D

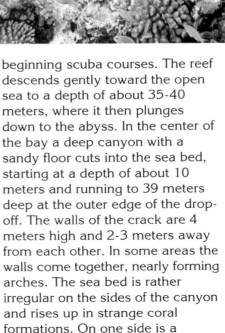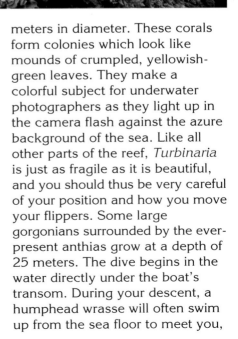

B

beginning scuba courses. The reef descends gently toward the open sea to a depth of about 35-40 meters, where it then plunges down to the abyss. In the center of the bay a deep canyon with a sandy floor cuts into the sea bed, starting at a depth of about 10 meters and running to 39 meters deep at the outer edge of the drop-off. The walls of the crack are 4 meters high and 2-3 meters away from each other. In some areas the walls come together, nearly forming arches. The sea bed is rather irregular on the sides of the canyon and rises up in strange coral formations. On one side is a spectacular cluster of Turbinaria mesenterina hard corals over 2

meters in diameter. These corals form colonies which look like mounds of crumpled, yellowish-green leaves. They make a colorful subject for underwater photographers as they light up in the camera flash against the azure background of the sea. Like all other parts of the reef, Turbinaria is just as fragile as it is beautiful, and you should thus be very careful of your position and how you move your flippers. Some large gorgonians surrounded by the ever-present anthias grow at a depth of 25 meters. The dive begins in the water directly under the boat's transom. During your descent, a humphead wrasse will often swim up from the sea floor to meet you, hoping for a hand-out. Never feed the fish, as this will increase their aggressiveness and change their eating habits. You could even kill them! When you reach the desired depth, go down into the canyon and explore it as you move back up. In shaded areas there are groupers lying in wait for possible prey, and a few other fish. The sunlight that reaches the sandy bottom forms beautiful shadows and plays of light. On the left side of the crack, at a depth of about 14 meters, is a low opening that widens out into a large cave. Aided by the beam of an underwater flashlight, you can explore the crevices populated by shrimp and other small crustaceans. It is not uncommon to see a large humphead wrasse approaching you confidently in the dark cavern. Coming out of the cavern, you will notice that the air bubbles you left on the vault of the cave pass through the porous corals toward the surface, forming a strange aquarium effect. At this point, keeping the wall to your left and staying at a depth of 12-15 meters, explore an area full of life, populated by schools of yellowfin goatfish and porgies with characteristic black stripes on their heads. If you want, you can go down to the wreck of a small boat lying overturned at a depth of 15 meters. This was a diving boat that sank in 1994 due to a fire on board. Scuba tanks and some metallic remains lie around the boat, and the population of glassfish that live under the stern are of some interest. Come back up to your starting point at a shallower depth, where the surroundings offer interesting subjects for photographers. Don't miss the red-tentacled anemone surrounded by tiny violet shrimp. Going a few meters beyond the place where the boat is moored, you'll find yourself on a sandy plateau from which dozens of little eels peep out, slowly withdrawing as you approach. Your ascent is aided by the mooring line, which you can grasp as you complete your decompression stop and watch the blue depths for swarms of passing fusiliers.

E

F

G

E - An encounter with a humphead wrasse (Cheilinus undulatus) is always a thrilling part of your dive. This large labridae is often accompanied by a jackfish, who uses its companion's massive body as cover in order to approach its prey unseen.

F - Scorpionfish (Scorpaenopsis oxycephala) are experts at the art of mimicry. They spend most of their time immobile on the reef lying in wait for their prey, which they capture in a rapid forward dart and suck into their large mouths.

G - A school of glassfish moving in compact formation before a diver is like an explosion of light. If you want to photograph these fish, remember that they are quite reflective, and keep your flash at the lowest setting.

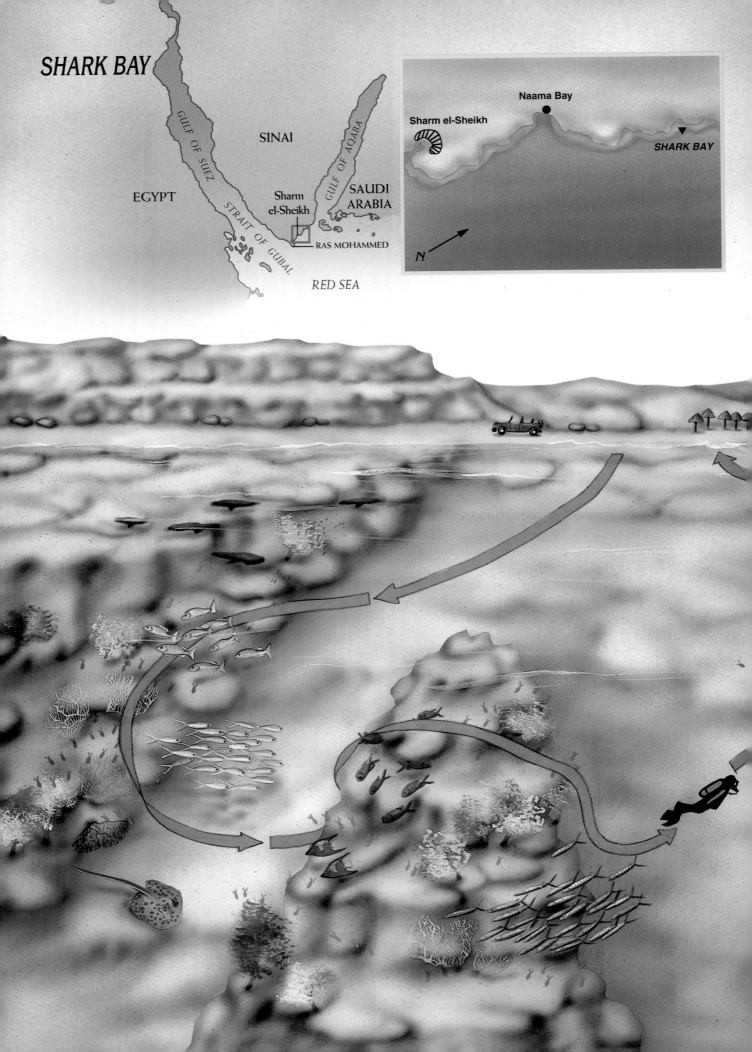

SHARK BAY

EGYPT · SINAI · SAUDI ARABIA

GULF OF SUEZ · GULF OF AQABA · STRAIT OF GUBAL

Sharm el-Sheikh · RAS MOHAMMED · RED SEA

Sharm el-Sheikh · Naama Bay · **SHARK BAY** · N

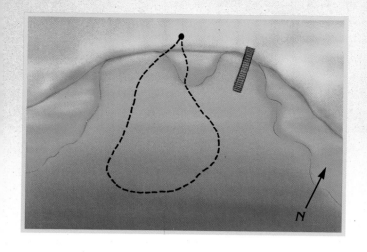

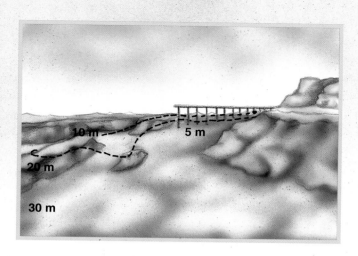

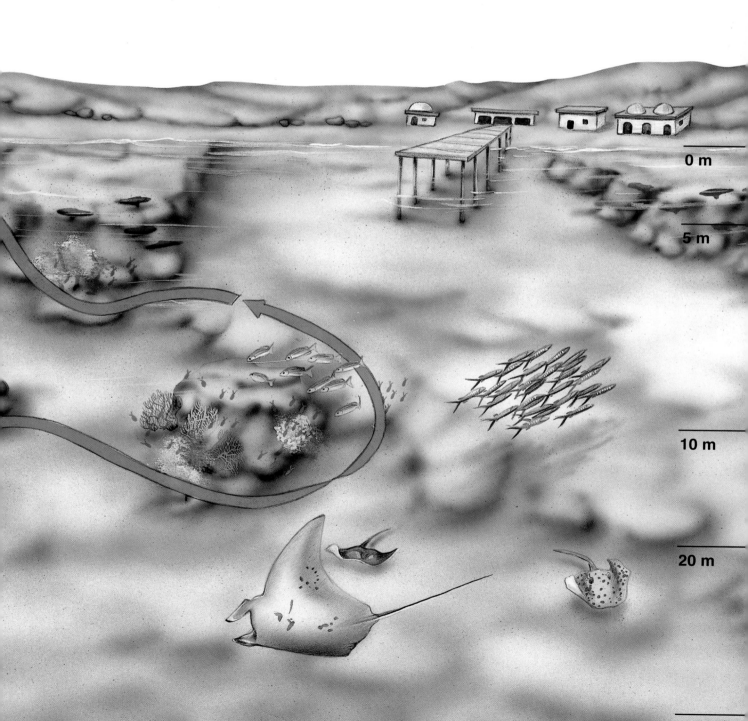

0 m

5 m

10 m

20 m

30 m

A

A - Dives at Shark Bay are quite easy, and being able to enter the water from the shore allows even divers who are a bit out of shape to gradually grow accustomed to the water.

B - You can dive at Shark Bay no matter what the weather, as the bay is deep and well-sheltered from the winds. After the dive, you can sample tasty local dishes at the restaurant just a few meters from the diving area.

C - If you explore the southern part of the gulf, you are likely to see a manta swimming with its mouth open against the flow of plankton transported by the water. These sightings are quite frequent during the winter months.

D - The stonefish (Synaceia verrucosa) is certainly the most skilled quick-change artist of all reef inhabitants. Due to its ability to take on the appearance of a small rock, it passes completely unnoticed by divers. Its dorsal fin is armed with sturdy spines connected to poison sacs that can cause extremely painful stings and other unpleasant complications: you should carefully examine the sea bed every time you need to stand on it.

E - In the early morning, dense groups of young barracudas gather on the shallow sandy sea beds near the pier, where they swim in circles.

B

C

D

Shark Bay is a 40 minute sail north of the port of Naama Bay. Although no sharks live in Shark Bay, its name comes from the fact that at one time local fishing boats moored in the bay often left the bodies of the sharks they caught to dry on the beach. You can also get here overland from Naama. Taking the road from the airport, after about 4 kilometers you'll see signs and the right turn that leads to the sea. This is a deep inlet, protected from winds and currents, where you can dive no matter what the weather conditions are. Environmental conditions make Shark Bay a perfect training area for beginner scuba divers, and hundreds of people have their

E

first, unforgettable experience diving with tanks in these warm, transparent waters. Usually you dive in directly from the shore, where the sandy bottom descends gently and there are small clusters of corals. On the right side of the inlet the bottom enlarges into a deep canyon with steep sides over 40 meters deep. Despite its popularity, the area still offers many good dives. You'll see numerous stingrays, who find an excellent habitat on the sea floor with the crustaceans and worms they like to eat. If you carefully explore the detrital areas, you'll see numerous stonefish, champions of mimicry who remain half-buried in the substratum, waiting for prey which they will suck into their large mouths. The stonefish is the most poisonous fish in the world, and it is thus extremely dangerous to touch them in order to make them move, as their poisonous spines could seriously injure you. Always remember that you should never touch anything in the water!

The sea beds of Shark Bay contain a true rarity: in some cavities you can see pipefish, strange little animals that change color to match their surroundings and are truly difficult to spot. Dense schools of small barracudas can be seen in the tranquil waters of the bay, where young individuals spend their time on the shallow sea beds.

Sometimes the current will carry large amounts of plankton into the bay, and it is not uncommon to see giant mantas, their large cephalic fins folded, gliding elegantly near the surface. You can take many entertaining night dives at Shark Bay, when you will see small, colored, almost phosphorescent cuttlefish, octopuses, crabs and many tiny creatures who will fascinate underwater photographers. This dive is certainly excellent for macrophotography, and good results are possible with extension tubes and underwater lenses like the 105 mm or the 60 mm. Be very careful not to stir up suspended particles, which will appear in the photo as white dots. In any case, you should angle your flash against the subject as much as possible.

F - A diver is exploring a section of the reef where hard corals as well as alcyonarians, sponges and many other life forms proliferates.

G - A blue-spotted stingray (Taeniura lymma) rests on a sandy clearing in the reef. During the day, these primarily nocturnal animals take shelter under plate coral formations or within small cracks in the wall.

H - A night dive always holds pleasant surprises: even a reef which looks uninteresting by day will certainly be full of brightly colored subjects by night, like this rare metallic-colored cuttlefish exploring the floor with its numerous tentacles.

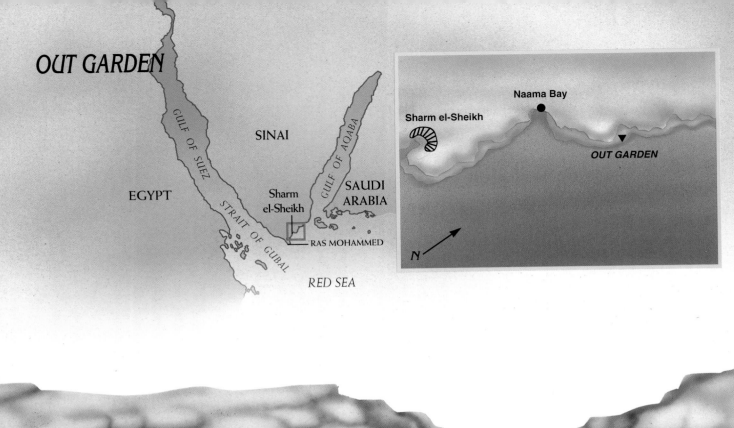

OUT GARDEN

GULF OF SUEZ

SINAI

EGYPT

GULF OF AQABA

SAUDI ARABIA

Sharm
el-Sheikh

STRAIT OF GUBAL

RAS MOHAMMED

RED SEA

Sharm el-Sheikh

Naama Bay

OUT GARDEN

N

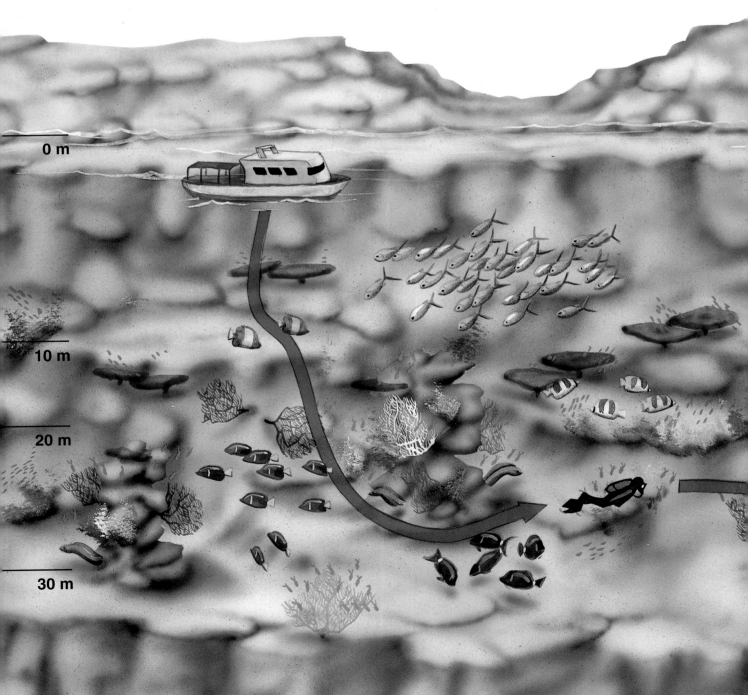

0 m

10 m

20 m

30 m

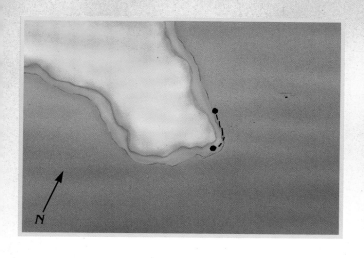

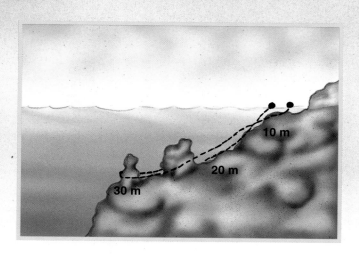

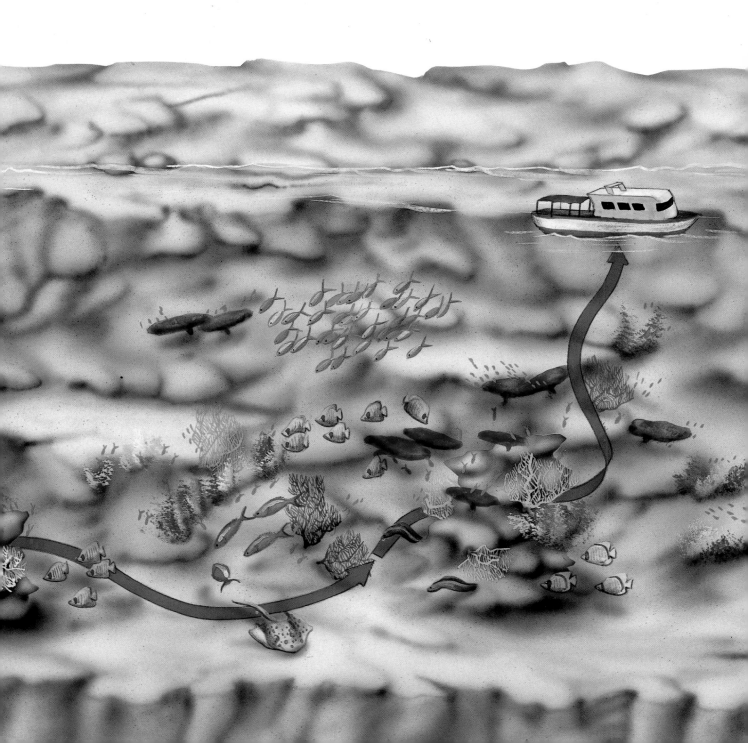

Head north from Naama Bay, and in a few minutes you'll come to the inlet which borders Far Garden to the north. After doubling the last of the "gardens," the coastline heads due north, and a few meters beyond the head the coast's high profile is interrupted, becoming a small beach with a deep *wadi*, or waterway that once flowed into the sea, behind it. The dive begins about 50 meters south of the small beach. There are no permanent mooring lines here, so the only way to explore Out Garden is through a drift dive. I recommend trying this dive during the afternoon when the wind drops and sea conditions are perfect, with the afternoon sun

C

A

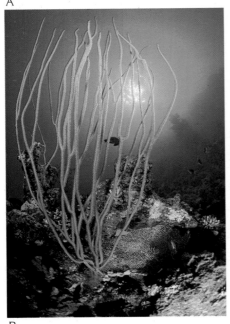

D

B

fully illuminating the sea floor. A gentle current usually runs north in the afternoon, making movement easier. This dive is not particularly difficult and is suitable for anyone. Dive in from the boat and descend to a plateau which descends at various angles to reach the drop-off at a depth of about 30 meters. Various tower-shaped coral formations rise up toward the surface; around them swim parrotfish, surgeonfish, butterflyfish and all sorts of other reef fish. Large morays can often be seen at the base of the pinnacles, as they allow cleaner fish to groom them. Gorgonians reach out to the current in the open sea, so that their fans come into contact with plankton.

The delicate lacework of these anthozoans hides a microfauna that includes hawkfish, gobies and small crustaceans that will be a joy for macrophotography buffs. Because these animals are quite shy, you should use an amphibious camera with a 105 mm lens, so you can stay some distance from your subjects. Large alcyonarians grow densely, and in some areas tumble down like cascades of flowers from a single coral spike. Cleaner fish have transformed the tops of some coral mushrooms into cleaning stations, and you can see various types and sizes of fish stopping there to be cleaned of parasites and organic remains. In the open waters, you'll see dense schools of fusiliers, always pursued by their predators: tunas and jacks. In the detrital areas you'll see blue-spotted stingrays partially buried in the sand. During the last part of the dive, you'll ascend along the wall, where there are deep vertical cracks rising up to the surface. In them you'll see masses of golden glassfish and groupers lying in wait in the shadows. The recommended depth is between 15 and 20 meters, keeping in mind that most sea life will be found around the summits of the pinnacles. Photographers can use this dive to capture shots of fish in their natural surroundings. The best lenses to use are standard, from 28 to 50 mm.

A, B - This wall, not often frequented by divers, contains gorgonians and sea whips in various sizes with particularly bright colors. The position of the reef, which is always swept by currents, creates ideal conditions for a regular inflow of plankton, permitting the corals to grow luxuriantly. These photos show a whip conformation with red-orange branches extended upward (above), and another delicate, bright red branch (below).

C - The emperor angelfish (Pomacanthus imperator) is very easy to photograph. As it is territorial, when a diver approaches it will retreat into a protected area of its territory, only to come out again after just a few moments. This magnificent coral fish emits loud snapping noises when it senses danger.

F

G

H

I

D - A close-up of a parrotfish (Scarus sordidus) among the corals. Parrotfish are diurnal and are a common sight along the reefs of the Red Sea. They feed on algae which they take from hard corals, along with their polyps and calcareous portions.

E - For the best shots of the large tangles of gorgonians fans, use a wide-angle lens, or, better yet, a fish-eye lens with a large field of vision that will allow you to come quite close to the subject.

F - The colorful emperor angelfish (Pomacanthus imperator) further adorns the already brightly-colored reefs of the Sinai coast.

G - The summits of coral pinnacles rising up from the sea floor are embellished by rich blooms of delicate alcyonarians in a thousand colors. Hundreds of fish of all sizes swim among its blossoms: here a red grouper (Cephalopholis miniata), ready to beat a hasty retreat, watches the photographer curiously .

H - The shallower part of the wall is broken by cracks that contain swarms of glassfish who will retreat to the deepest part of the crevices if approached too quickly.

I - This blue-spotted stingray was photographed during a night dive as it was digging in the detrital floor in search of worms and shrimp. These stingrays move with the high tide, usually during the evening hours.

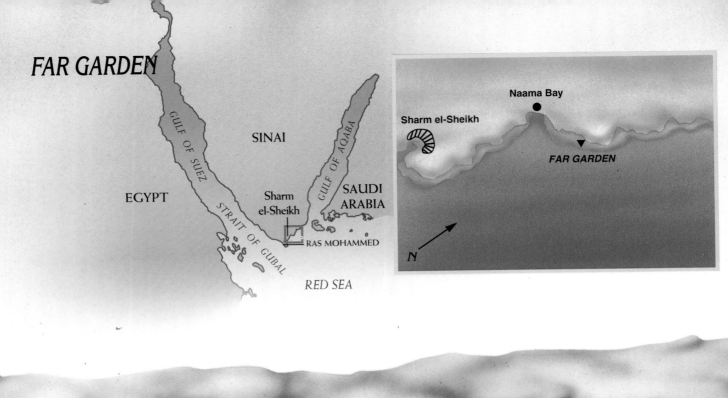

FAR GARDEN

GULF OF SUEZ

SINAI

GULF OF AQABA

EGYPT

STRAIT OF GUBAL

Sharm
el-Sheikh

SAUDI
ARABIA

RAS MOHAMMED

RED SEA

Sharm el-Sheikh

Naama Bay

FAR GARDEN

N

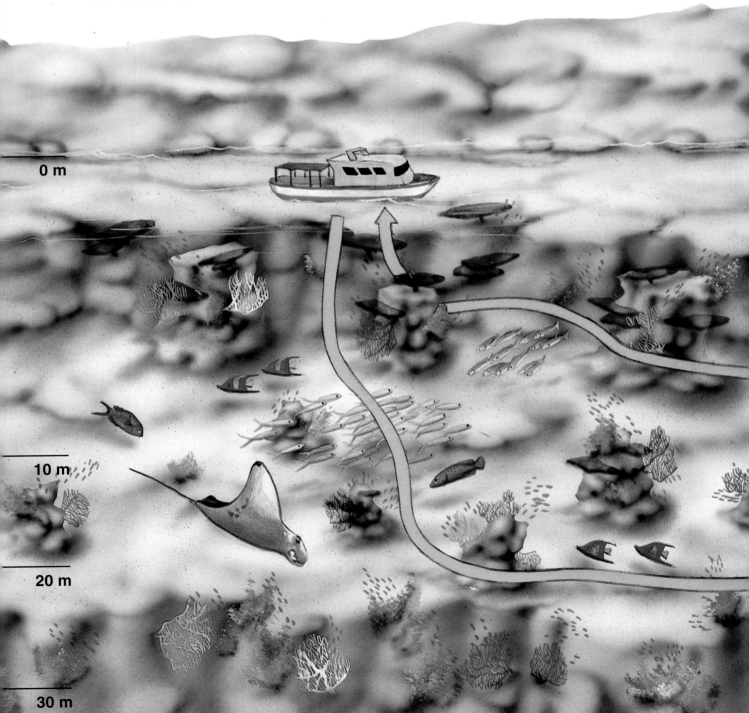

0 m

10 m

20 m

30 m

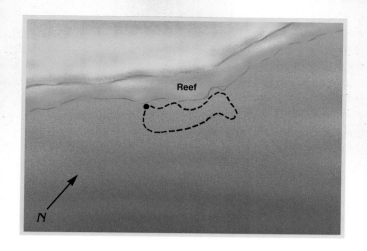

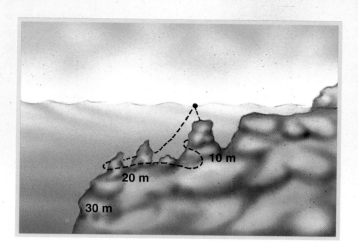

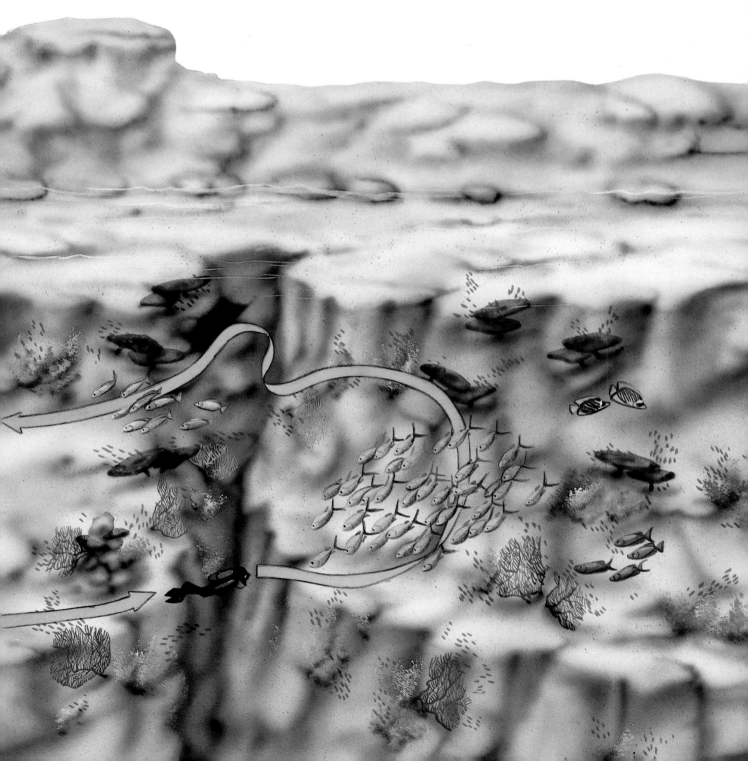

A - This photograph shows the rhythmic pulse of the underwater world: hundreds of tiny anthias (Pseudanthias squamipinnus) swim alongside each other around soft corals in a thousand forms and colors.

B - This anthias is in the process of a sexual transformation from female to male. The small fish still has the classic orange color of the female, but has already developed a long dorsal fin and a violet spot on its pectoral fins, clear signs of a male.

C - A pair of striped cardinal fish (Cheilodipterus quinquelineatus) rest on a Porites coral. Usually cardinal fish are associated with long-spined urchins, among whose spines they take refuge in case of danger.

D - A splendid example of a whitetip reef shark (Triaedon obesus) curiously approaches, scrutinizing the divers with its small eyes.

A

B

C

D

Far Garden is about a 15 minute sail north of Naama Bay. It is the northernmost of the three coral gardens in a wide inlet. This dive is suitable for both beginners and more expert divers, and despite its relative proximity to Naama Bay, the area still offers extremely interesting, lively sea beds. A nighttime dive at Far Garden will reveal so many subjects that even the most hardened underwater photographers will be impressed. The shallower portion of the reef is easy to explore by snorkelers, and is full of corals and brightly colored fish. Moor your boat using one of the two permanent mooring lines that are

E

firmly tied at a depth of about 25 meters. Alternatively, if you are skilled enough, you can use drift dive techniques. From the surface, the walls of the reef descend vertically to a depth of 4-5 meters. This is the realm of anthias, who move in unison away from the wall, to return suddenly if any potential predator approaches. The sea bed then descends to a wide terrace which drops steeply to a depth of 25 meters, where it plunges into the abyss in a vertical wall. On the plateau, up to the drop-off, there are numerous pinnacles that in some cases rise nearly to the surface. A large variety of fish swims around these coral towers, including butterflyfish, parrotfish, schools of yellow goatfish and red groupers. On the side facing the open sea, where they are better exposed to the current, there are large gorgonians and thick tufts of soft corals. Clusters of black corals like weeping willows grow where the wall plunges into deepest blue depths. This is near a point that extends into the open sea, and you should thus look out into the open water from time to time, where you may see tunas and jacks passing, and perhaps even a whitetip shark. Especially in the winter, when the current carries plankton into the bay, you may find yourself swimming in the company of a giant manta gliding elegantly along the reef. An encounter with one of these giants of the sea is always a wonderful and thrilling experience.

Photographers will need to choose their lenses depending on the type of subjects they want to capture. If you want a seascape shot around the pinnacles, with gorgonians, alcyonarians and sponges, use a wide-angle lens like the 15 mm. Because the water is so clear, pelagic fish swimming in the open sea can be photographed using a 28 mm or 35 mm lens mounted on a *Nikonos*, even without a flash. For macrophotographers, the best results will be obtained using lenses like the 60 or 105 mm mounted on a camera in an underwater case. Because operating depth is somewhat shallow, environmental light is rather strong, and you can use low sensitivity film like the 50 or 64 ASA.

Once you enter the water, you can use the mooring line as a landmark for your descent, and once you have reached the desired depth, begin your dive, keeping the drop-off to your right and heading north. After you've explored around the deeper coral towers, ascend to examine the cavities of the pinnacles, rising up from a depth of 10 meters. After you visit the small glassfish cave, which is in the wall at a depth of 4 meters, end your dive near the reef and swim back to the boat from the surface.

E - Grunts and snappers, with their silver coloring reflecting the sun rays, often swim along the upper part of the reef, looking for prey.

F - Macrophotography fans will find an endless number of tiny subjects among the branches of the gorgonian sea fans, including pipefish, gobies, crabs, hawkfish and many other tiny animals.

G - Jacks (Caranx sp.) *are quite common in the Red Sea, and sometimes they gather in groups of hundreds of individuals. These tireless swimmers move continuously among the reefs in search of the small fish on which they feed.*

H

F

I

G

H - To get good shots of groups of glassfish, always consider the high reflective capacity of these small fish, and set the electronic camera flash accordingly.

I - Mantas come close to the reef only when they want cleaner fish to remove their parasites. Otherwise, they are pelagic fish which follow plankton migrations.

NEAR GARDEN

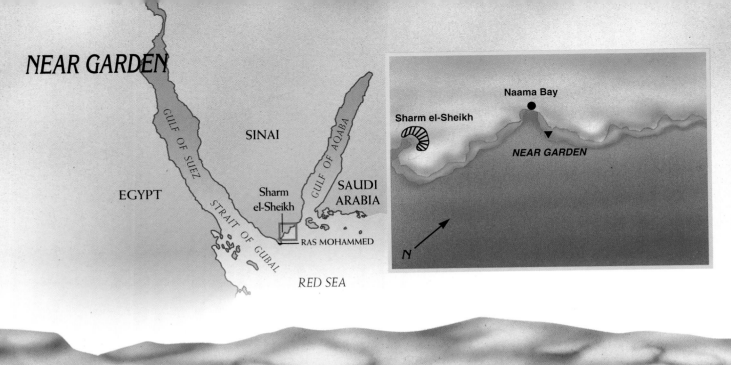

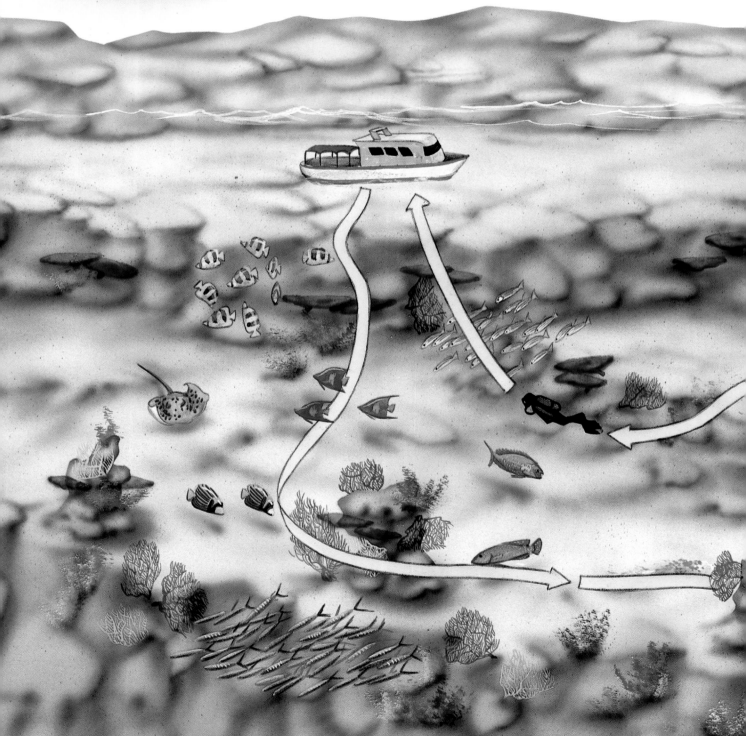

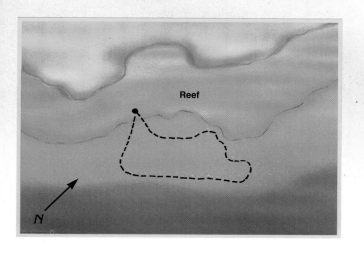

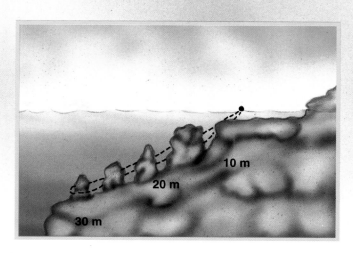

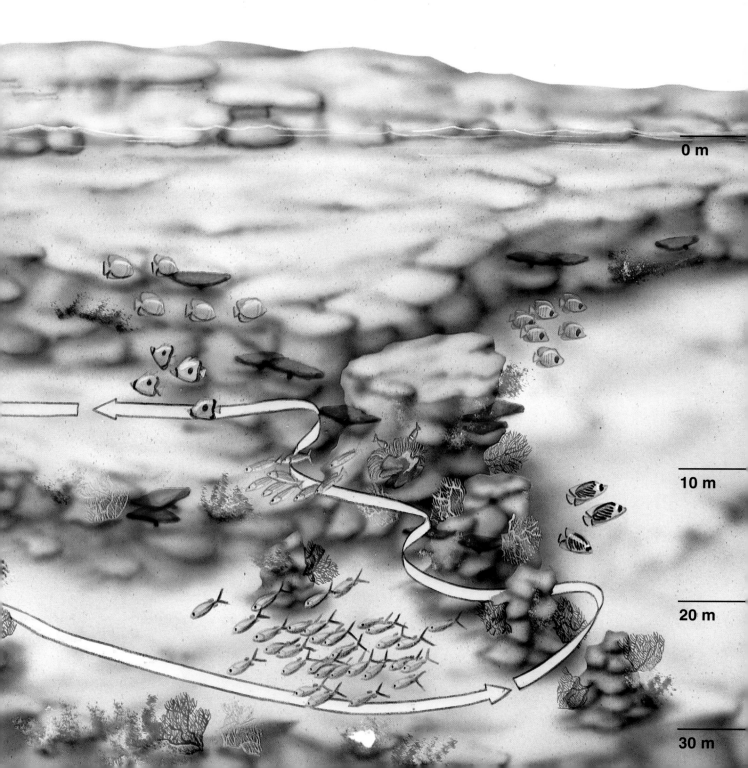

Reef

N

10 m

20 m

30 m

0 m

10 m

20 m

30 m

A - Crinoids with arms similar to delicate feathers are attached to the outside edge of a gorgonian. This echinoderm moves along the reef using sturdy filaments under its disk. While these animals rarely come out during the day, they are a constant sight during night dives, when they can be seen with their arms completely open as they convey plankton to their mouths. In the background are two young batfish.

B, C - Near the drop-off are coral towers where various types of alcyonarians and gorgonian sea fans grow alongside each other. Numerous Pterois miles *live among them. Moving furtively, this fish awaits any small prey that unwisely approaches its mouth, when it will rapidly dart forward and swallow it.*

C

A

B

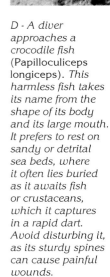

D

D - A diver approaches a crocodile fish (Papilloculiceps longiceps). This harmless fish takes its name from the shape of its body and its large mouth. It prefers to rest on sandy or detrital sea beds, where it often lies buried as it awaits fish or crustaceans, which it captures in a rapid dart. Avoid disturbing it, as its sturdy spines can cause painful wounds.

E - Hard corals grow in an endless variety of forms that never follow a set direction, but develop so that the greatest surface area possible is swept by the currents. Gorgonian sea fans and alcyonarians colonize the hard substrata, creating bright spots of color.

Leaving Naama Bay and sailing north, in a few minutes you'll reach a broad inlet which contains the three most famous diving areas in the region: Near, Middle and Far Gardens.

Near Garden is the best known, because it is continuously visited by glass-bottom boats that allow even those with no diving experience to discover the underwater marvels that this sea contains. The shallower part of the reef offers extremely interesting sights even for snorkelers, who will find themselves swimming among clouds of fish who are not disturbed by their presence in the slightest. Boats can moor at two permanent mooring lines not far from each other. I personally prefer to begin the dive from the more northerly line. Although the area is heavily trafficked, Near Garden still offers pleasant dives, especially for macro photographers. The area is also an extraordinary place for night dives, when you will see small crustaceans camouflaged among the alcyonarians, parrotfish enveloped in their cocoons and many other reef inhabitants who come out only at night.

From its surface edge, the reef descends 4-6 meters in a small vertical wall full of small crevices and hard corals, where you'll see butterflyfish, parrotfish and the ever-present anthias. The wall then descends gently to a depth of about 25 meters, where it turns into a vertical drop which is beyond the reach of recreational divers. On the plateau there are areas of sand mixed with sediments where you'll see blue-spotted stingrays partially buried in the sand as they await the night, when they'll move to the shallower parts of the reef in search of the shrimp and worms on which they feed. The crocodile fish is another frequent sight in mixed coral and sandy areas. This fish gets its name from the form of its body, especially its head, which it rests on the floor as it awaits prey that it captures in lightning-quick darts. The sea floor is broken by small coral towers on which grow luxuriant soft corals and

E

anemones. The coral peaks reach their maximum splendor at the drop-off, where you'll see large gorgonian fans reaching into the blue depths, and trees of black corals that offer shelter to small transparent glassfish and groups of young cardinal fish. If you look carefully around these formations, you'll see numerous turkeyfish lying in wait, with all their fins characteristically folded back along their body so that their prey will not see them. This part of the reef offers many areas suitable for wide-angle lenses. The gorgonians and the alcyonarians can be captured at close range using backlight techniques, perhaps with the silhouette of a diver standing out on the sea floor. When you explore the outside edge of the wall, don't forget to look out to the open sea, where you may see pelagic fish like tunas and jacks passing by. This dive begins as you descend along the mooring line to which your boat is anchored. When you reach a depth of 20-25 meters, proceed south, keeping the drop-off to your left. When you come to a large formation of black corals and gorgonians, begin your ascent, following the terrain of the sea floor. End your dive as you explore the little wall 4-6 meters deep. You should always emerge near the reef and swim to the boat from the surface.

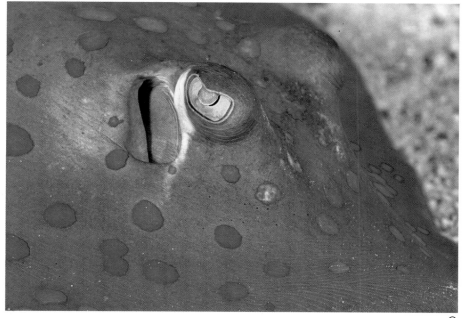
F

F - The sandy and detrital areas of the reef are the realm of blue-spotted stingrays (Taeniura lymma), which patrol the flat areas in search of food.

G - A pale violet shrimp appears among the vesicles of a grape coral (Plerogyra sinuosa). Plerogyra grows in colonies characterized by protective vesicles which retract when the animal is touched.

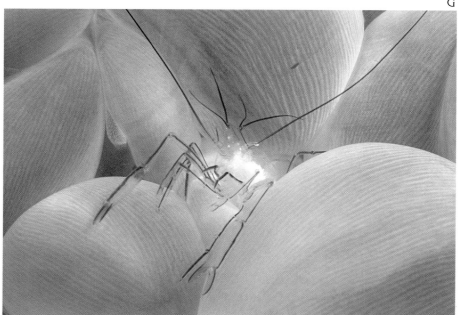
G

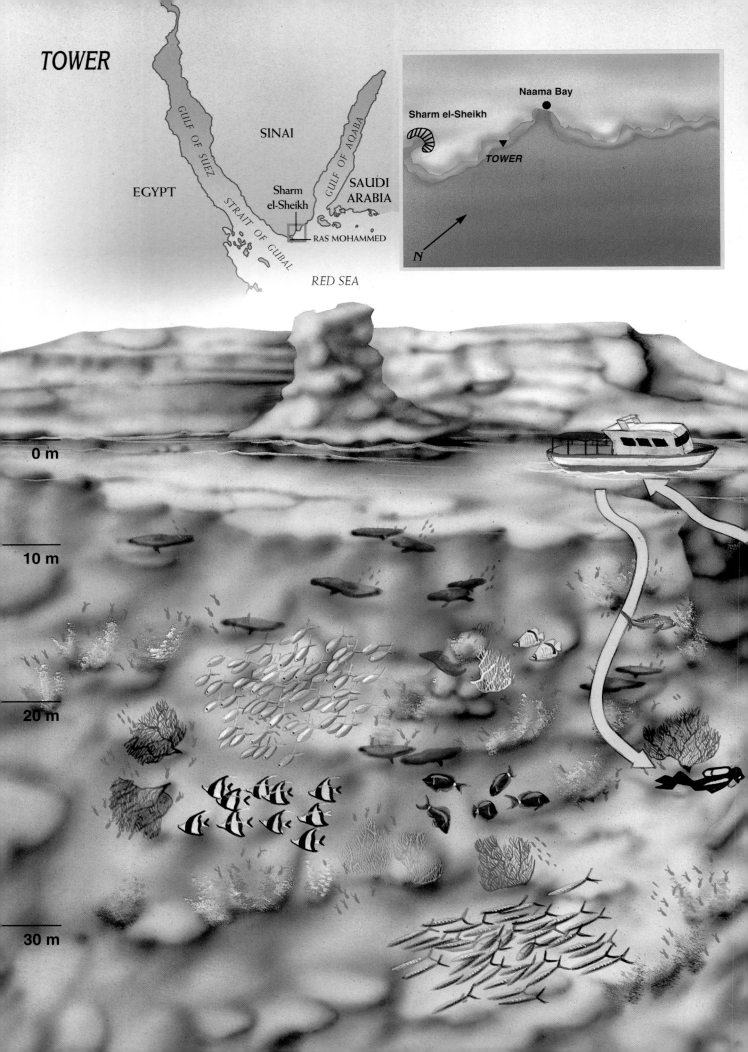

TOWER

GULF OF SUEZ

SINAI

GULF OF AQABA

EGYPT

STRAIT OF GUBAL

Sharm el-Sheikh

SAUDI ARABIA

RAS MOHAMMED

RED SEA

Naama Bay

Sharm el-Sheikh

TOWER

N

0 m

10 m

20 m

30 m

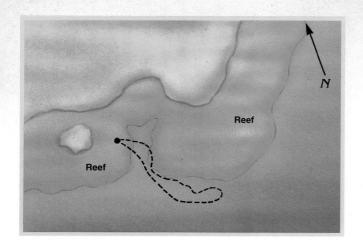

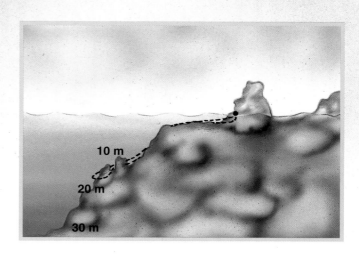

Reef

Reef

N

10 m

20 m

30 m

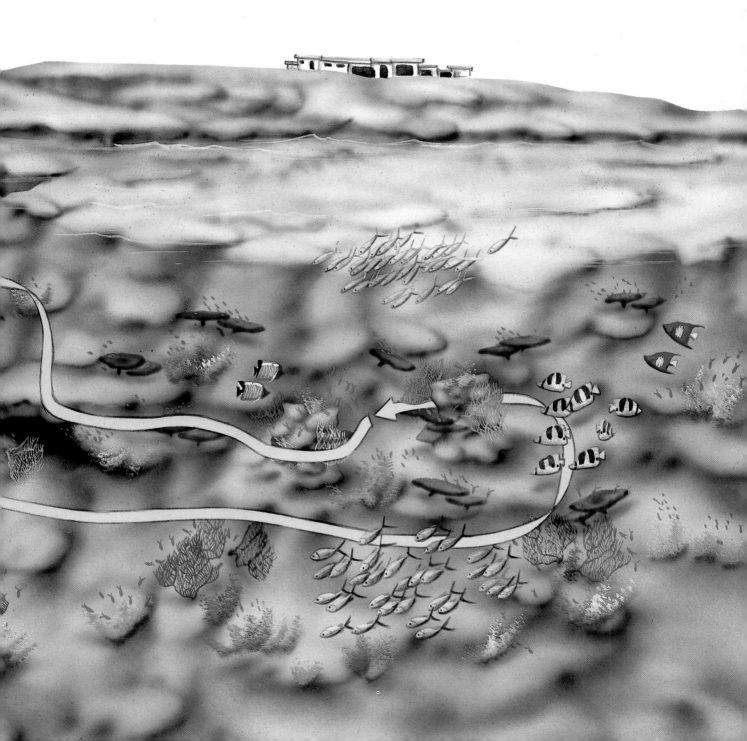

A - A group of
bluefin trevallies
(Caranx
melampygus)
follows a school
of fusiliers. These
predators are more
active in the early
morning and
shortly before dusk,
when they move
among the
protuberances
on the sea floor
and then dart into
the open water in
pursuit of their prey.

The first diving area south of Naama Bay is Tower. It is only a ten minute sail to the tower of rock standing out from the wall, which gives the area its name and borders a small bay to the south. This is one of the most interesting wall dives in the Naama Bay area and can be enjoyed by divers with any level of experience, provided you stay at the proper depth. There is no permanent mooring line that reaches the surface, so the divemaster must dive in to anchor the boat to a sharp projection of dead coral on the

C

A

B

D

right side of the canyon. Another alternative is a drift dive to the north. In either case, you should dive at Tower only when weather conditions are perfect. Evidently, at one time a watercourse flowed into this area, and the structure of the underwater wall shows the effects. The reef near the *wadi* is furrowed by a deep canyon that vanishes into the depths. The walls of the gorge are quite steep, and at shallow depths do not offer much to see. Within the small bay, at a depth of 5 meters, is a cave opening into the wall with

B - Alcyonarians are certainly some of the most colorful corals you will see during your dives in the Sharm el-Sheikh area. Looking like flowering bushes, they grow one on top of another all along the coral reef, gracing it with their lively colors and extraordinary forms.

an exit in the upper part of the reef. The dive begins here, and after a visit to the cave you'll move along the north wall of the canyon to a depth of 25 meters. At this point, keeping the wall to your left, head north, where the corals increase. There are many pinnacles on a steep detrital plateau, surrounded by alcyonarians and gorgonians. Pairs of butterflyfish swim slowly by, while colorful parrotfish are intent on breaking off pieces of coral with their strong beaks, and several lionfish rest on the hard corals, trying to camouflage themselves as much as possible. The view is enlivened by anthias swimming everywhere; these small predators move jerkily in a rhythmic dance as they follow the zooplankton on which they feed. In addition to watching the colorful show of reef fish, you should also keep your eye on the open sea, where swarms of fusiliers swim, pursued by jackfish. The jacks move swiftly through the ranks of these small fish, trying to isolate one and thus make it easier prey. Move a couple of meters from the wall to circle a coral tower from which clusters of alcyonarians hang into the void. Beneath you the wall descends vertically and the water is crystalline. Under these circumstances, it is always best to check your wrist instruments to avoid being lured by the fascination of the drop-off. Now it's time to begin surfacing, and you'll move to between 10 and 15 meters deep, where the coral mushrooms are especially full of life; the light is intense and the beauty of the seascape draws photographers. Even the fish seem to pose to help make your photos perfect. The last few meters of the reef, near the surface, are a discovery as well: a group of yellow goatfish with blue-striped snouts frenetically scours the reef with long barbels, digging out the small fish on which they feed. They are so engrossed in their work that it is easy to approach them for beautiful close-ups. The depth of the dive at Tower often reaches the limits of recreational diving, and thus you should never forget your 5 minute safety decompression stop at a depth of 5 meters.

C - The great fans of the gorgonians are a sort of natural barrier against the current, providing a shelter for creatures like turkeyfish, which are not very streamlined and thus do not like moving water.

D - A sharksucker (Echeneis naucrates) is attached to a large batfish (Platax orbicularis). Sharksuckers, which rarely swim alone, use a sucker on the upper part of the head to attach to the body of large fish such as sharks and mantas or turtles, who then carry them as they swim.

G

E

H

F

E - The silhouette of a diver stands out against the sun. A gorgonian in the foreground has extended its polyps, making it look like a frozen tree.

F - This superb orange alcyonarian is extending its polyps in order to filter as much plankton as possible from the water.

G - The sunlight that filters down from above highlights the complex branching formation of what looks like a petrified tree. Branching and umbrella-shaped colonies are characteristic of the Acropora family.

H - A pair of crinoids extend their feathered arms toward the open sea to feed on the particles of plankton carried by the current.

PINKY'S WALL

EGYPT

SINAI

GULF OF SUEZ

GULF OF AQABA

SAUDI ARABIA

STRAIT OF GUBAL

Sharm el-Sheikh

RAS MOHAMMED

RED SEA

Naama Bay

Sharm el-Sheikh

PINKY'S WALL

N

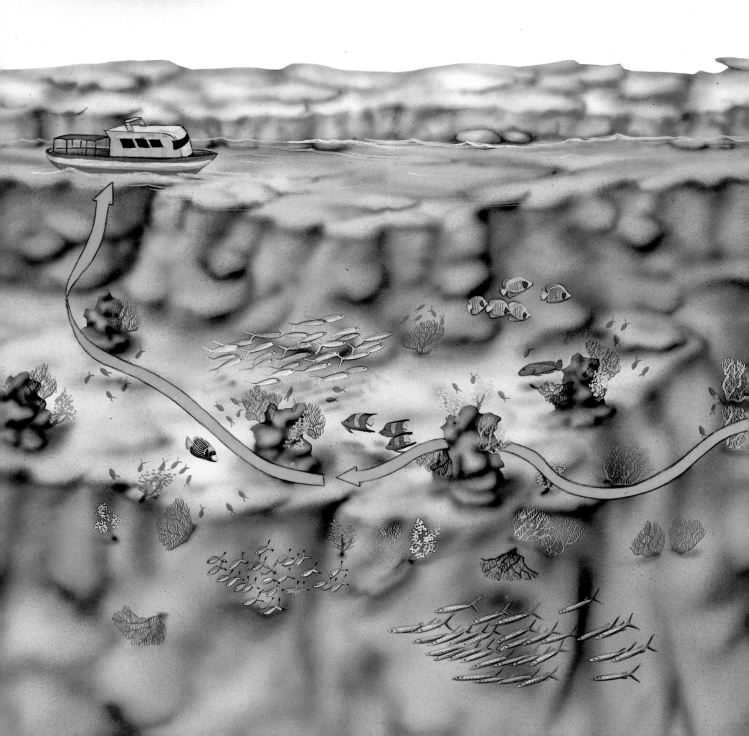

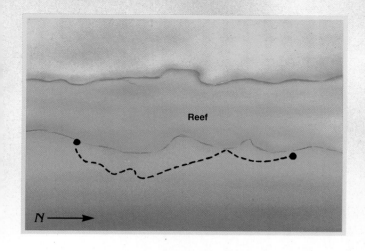

Reef

N →

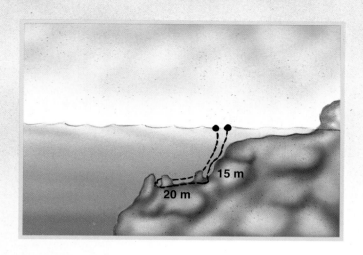

15 m

20 m

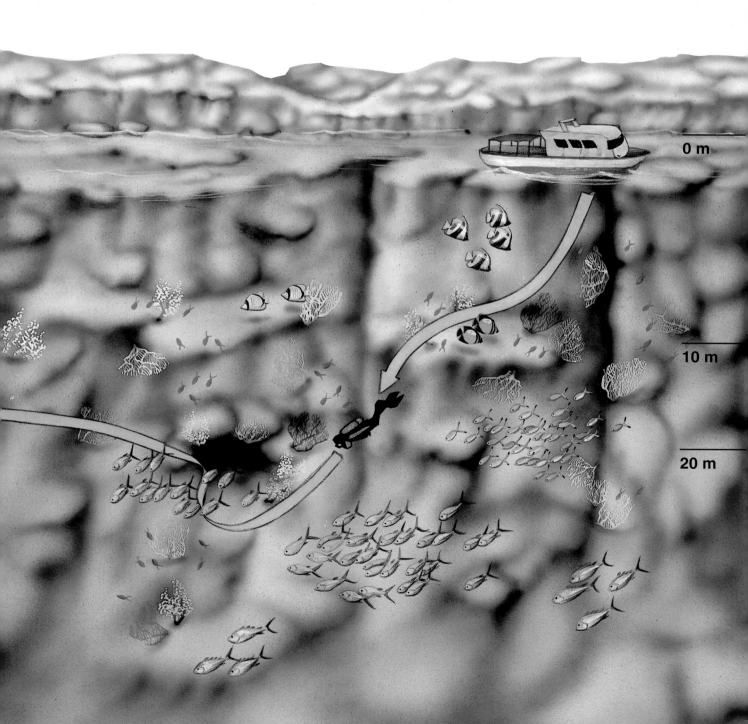

0 m

10 m

20 m

Pinky's Wall is halfway between the two ports of Sharm el-Maya and Naama Bay, a little over 20 minutes from either port. The diving area, located between Tower and Paradise, is a wall that plunges into the blue depths of the sea. The reef is broken by vertical cracks, and crevices dot the wall. This is a classic wall dive, as the coral wall drops away as far as the eye can see right from the surface, and even when you reach your depth limits you cannot see the bottom. You should frequently check your instruments during this excursion so that you will not be deceived by the transparency of the water and find yourself deeper than you intended to go. There are no

C

A

B

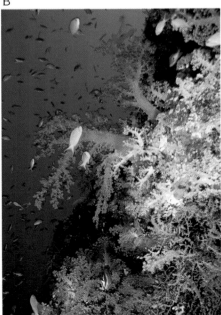

D

A - The growth of gorgonians is always influenced by the currents. By positioning themselves perpendicular to the walls, all their polyps will be ensured a constant supply of water full of nourishment and oxygen.

B, C - Flowering alcyonarians embellish the steep sides of Pinky's Wall, with an exceptionally large group of anthias close by. Groups of this small fish, which may be orange to violet in color, are only seemingly chaotic: they include territorial males surrounded by immature individuals and a harem of females.

permanent mooring lines in the area, so a drift dive will be necessary. Before you enter the water, be sure the sea conditions are perfect so you will have no difficulty getting back on board. Enter the water a little north of a break in the coastline that permits access to the sea from the shore as well. You should head south during the dive, keeping the wall to your right until you reach the area known as "Amphoras". Pinky's Wall gets its name from the bushes of alcyonarians that embellish the wall: at a depth of 15 to 20 meters, true cascades of soft corals in colors that range from pink to countless shades of lilac decorate every projection on the reef. When the water carries in nourishment, the alcyonarians burst into full flower, extending the white polyps of their feathered tentacles. If you look carefully among the flowers, you will see small gobies and tiny crustaceans moving among the branches of these delicate bushes. As you approach the wall, be very careful not to touch anything, and watch any hanging equipment you may have as well, to avoid destroying in an instant what Nature took years to create. It will be difficult to take your eyes from the wall, but every so often you should glance out to the open water, where you may see dense schools of fusiliers followed by solitary tunas and groups of jacks. Within the roughest crevices, you will see swarms of glassfish closely eyed by redmouth groupers. At a certain point during your dive, at a depth of between 15 and 20 meters, you will notice that the wall extends toward the open water in a sort of plateau, with its outside edge covered by sea fans. When you reach this point, cross this terrace diagonally and circle around low coral towers that teem with the frenetic life of the reef: groups of butterflyfish that move only if divers come too close, angelfish intent on biting off tender sponges, groups of yellow goatfish that nervously move from one crevice to another, and many other reef inhabitants. When you reach your safety decompression depth, approach the wall before emerging and swim to the boat from the surface.

D - Jacks swim in the open water not far from the reef. While hunting, these fast pelagic fish use a strategy similar to that used by wolf packs: they surround the schools of fish, forcing them against the wall and cutting off any flight toward the open sea, then two or three individuals at a time make the final attack, driving into the school of now frightened small fish.

E - A couple of bannerfish (Heniochus diphreutes) swim together with two yellow masked butterflyfish (Chaetodon semilarvatus), not far from a fire coral formation (Millepora dichotoma).

E

G

H

F - As you dive along these reefs, you will be struck by the variety of animal forms which coexist in such a limited space. Everyone's final goal is to stake out a territory where they can find food, and to defend it to create optimal conditions for reproduction.

G - Angelfish, like this Pomacanthus imperator, have small mouths armed with teeth they use to break off the sponges and soft corals on which they feed.

H - A group of black-spotted grunts (Plectorhynchus gaterinus) hovers in the shelter of a coral tower. During the day, these bright yellow, spotted reef inhabitants usually gather under umbrella coral formations.

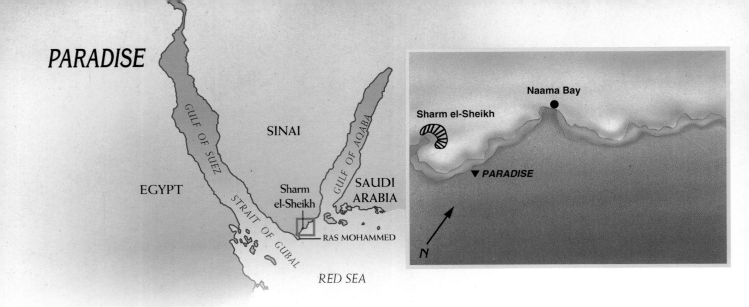

PARADISE

SINAI

EGYPT

GULF OF SUEZ

GULF OF AQABA

SAUDI
ARABIA

Sharm
el-Sheikh

STRAIT OF GUBAL

RAS MOHAMMED

RED SEA

Sharm el-Sheikh

Naama Bay

PARADISE

N

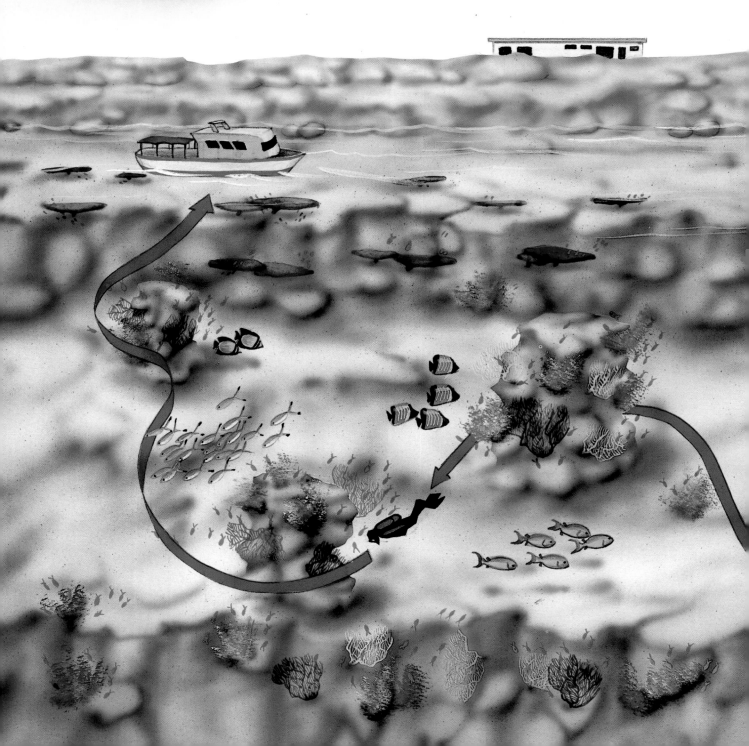

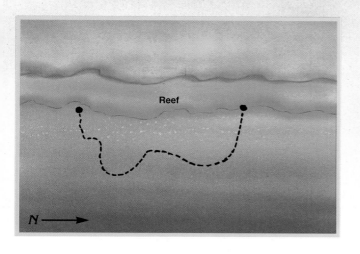

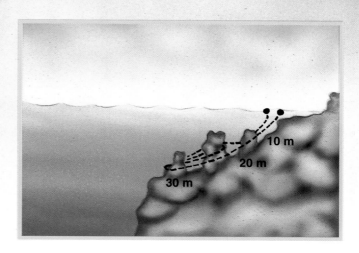

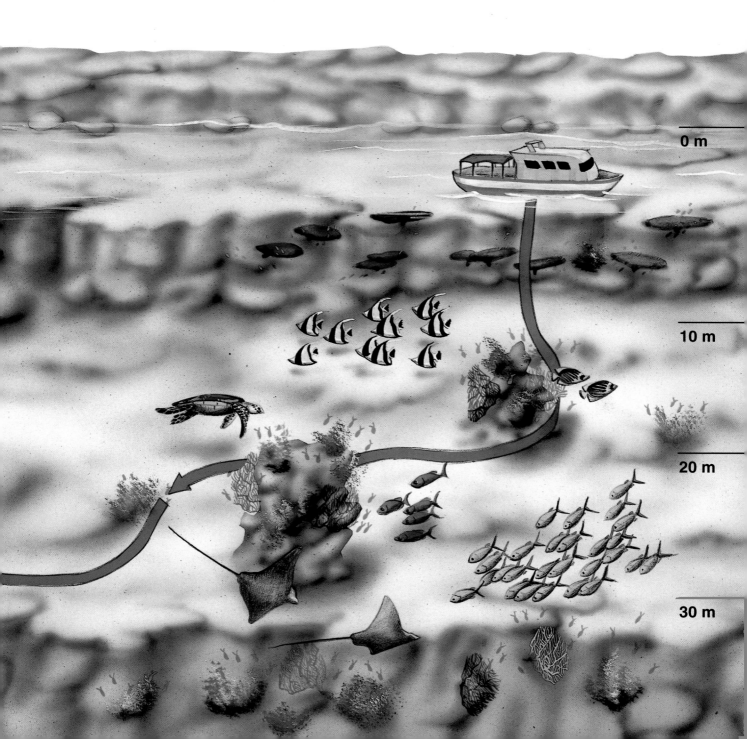

0 m

10 m

20 m

30 m

Reef

N

A

B

C

D

Paradise is about a 20 minute sail north of Sharm el-Maya. After doubling the cape of Ras um Sid, the coastline heads north to Tower, with almost no inlets. The sea beds in this area are more or less the same, with numerous little-known diving areas, perhaps because of the lack of permanent mooring lines and the relatively unsheltered position. The diving area known as "Paradise" stretches out between "Fiasco" and "Amphoras".
The reef descends from the surface in a vertical drop to 8-10 meters deep, where it then descends in a gentle slope to a depth of 25-30 meters, where the drop-off wall begins, plunging down vertically to the abyss. The explorable areas, located at various depths, contain coral pinnacles, some of which are 7-8 meters high and 2 meters wide, which make you feel as if you were moving through the columns of a portico. As this is a drift dive, you should descend only when weather conditions are excellent, to avoid problems when you come back up to the boat. When there are no waves, the dive is not particularly difficult and is suitable for divers with all levels of skill, as long as they have some experience in diving in currents. Begin the dive from the boat about 50 meters north of a low structure you can see from the mainland, and proceed south, keeping the wall to your right. Just a few meters deep you'll see strange coral formations which are home to parrotfish and families of butterflyfish, while small clumps of *Turbinaria* corals create beautiful spots of yellow-green.
The coral towers scattered about at a depth of 20-25 meters are covered with various types of brightly colored gorgonians and clusters of red sponges. The soft corals and sponges reach their maximum splendor near the top of the pinnacles, where they are surrounded by swarms of brilliant glassfish. Some formations are real explosions of life and color: deep violent gorgonians with white expanded polyps look like frozen bushes, standing right next to a red cascade of sponges alive with slow-moving yellow and black nudibranchs, and alcyonarians are everywhere, in every imaginable color: violet, pink, and scarlet, filling any empty spaces. Often the upper portion of these formations is embellished with umbrella corals more than two meters wide, among whose branches large schools of jerkily-moving green damselfish take refuge.
On the plateau, in the areas the corals have not covered, you can see crocodile fish and spotted stingrays half-buried in the sand. As this area is near Ras um Sid,

A - The long branches of red whip corals extend up toward the surface. A careful inspection of their filaments will reveal numerous small animals who find protection among the tangles.

B - Spectacular yellow and black nudibranchs often move along the branches of this type of sponge, creating marvelous opportunities for macrophotography fans.

C - Paradise may capture the fantasy of underwater photographers more than any other dive. The red encrusting sponges, the gorgonians covered by alcyonarians and the sociable fish truly do make it a paradise where you can dive dozens of times and still find new things to photograph.

D - Near the surface, the coral blocks reach extraordinary dimensions and look like true mountains.

E

E - A solitary butterflyfish (Chaetodon melannotus) swims among the corals. Butterflyfish almost always live in pairs near the branching corals on whose polyps they feed. Note the black band on the snout that hides the eyes: this protects the fish from predators, who cannot distinguish the head from the rest of the body.

F

F - What seems like a petrified gorgonian is actually an umbrella coral growing in a way that permits each part to receive enough sunlight for its symbiotic algae.

G - This small white-bellied damselfish (Amblyglyphidodon leucogaster) is extremely territorial and will not hesitate to attack and bite anyone, including divers, who come too close to its home.

G

H

you may see pelagic fish like jackfish, tunas and eagle rays. At the end of your dive, as you ascend along the wall to your safety stop, you'll see turtles swimming slowly near the reef in search of food.

The person who called this place "Paradise" was probably an underwater photographer. Recommended lenses for this dive are certainly wide-angles like the 15 mm or 18 mm, or fisheye lenses like the 16 mm, which you can use to capture large frames while still staying quite close to your subject. The shallow depth allows you to work in mixed light, using medium sensitivity film.

I

H - An encounter with an eagle ray (Aetobatus narinari) is always exciting; sometimes you may see groups of a dozen individuals passing by. These rays are ovoviviparous, giving birth to one to four baby rays after a twelve month gestation period.

I - The leafy conformation of Turbinaria corals makes them easy to identify from other corals. The constructor polyps prove what colors and bizarre shapes they are capable of.

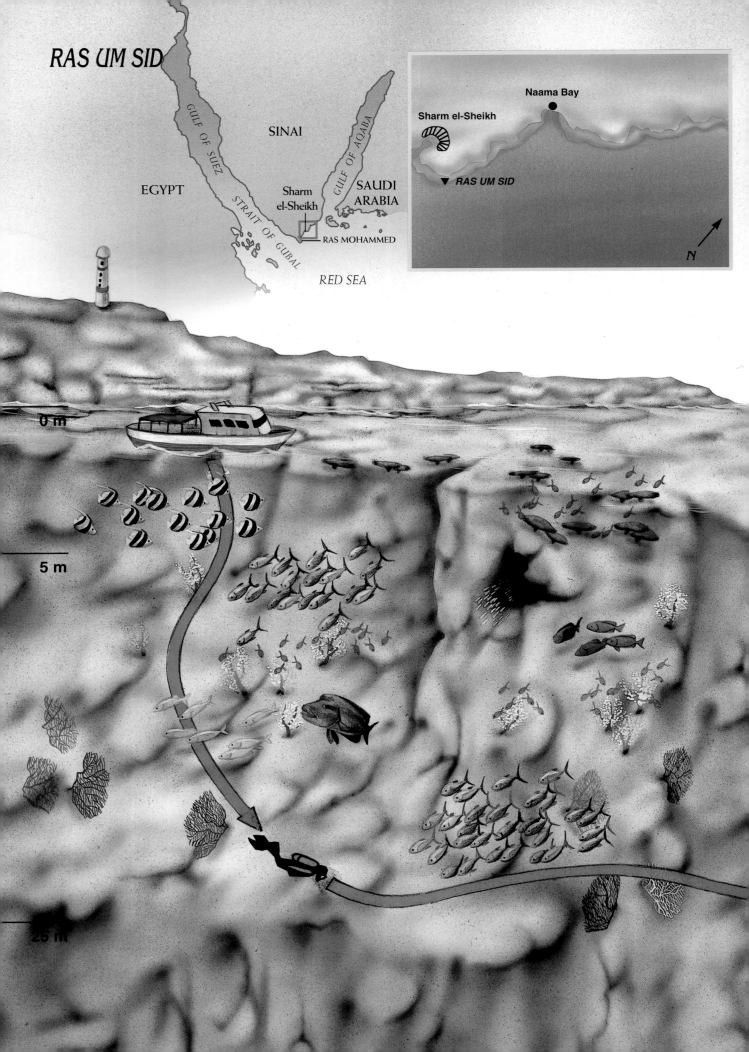

RAS UM SID

SINAI

GULF OF SUEZ

GULF OF AQABA

STRAIT OF GUBAL

EGYPT

SAUDI ARABIA

Sharm el-Sheikh

RAS MOHAMMED

RED SEA

Naama Bay

Sharm el-Sheikh

RAS UM SID

N

0 m

5 m

25 m

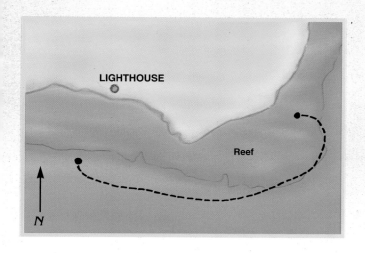

LIGHTHOUSE

Reef

N

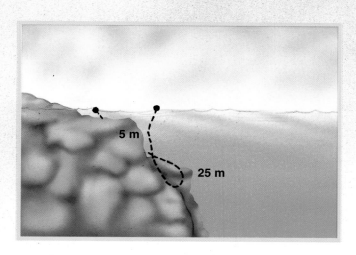

5 m

25 m

A - At Ras um Sid boats anchor in the northern part of the gulf under the lighthouse, where the floor descends vertically to a first terrace at about 20-25 meters deep. Boats can moor at two permanent mooring lines.

B - The gorgonian forest is one of the most spectacular attractions of this diving area.

Ras um Sid (in Arabic, *ras* means cape) is a promontory that juts out into the sea. The area is about a 15 minute sail north of the port of Sharm el-Maya. The diving area has two permanent mooring lines for boats. This dive is also possible from land, but it is certainly easier and more fun if you have a boat. This is one of the most spectacular places in the Sharm el-Sheikh area and is a real photographers' paradise. The reef descends vertically, broken by cracks and coral formations,

A

B

C

D

down to a depth of about 25 meters, where there is a narrow plateau which vanishes into the blackness of the deep waters. Large humphead wrasses are common here, and along the walls are small groups of yellow goatfish, along with various types of butterflyfish. Don't miss the small cave 5 meters deep, where there is a dense school of glassfish swimming among the large red and white alcyonarians. In the open sea there are fusiliers, and small pelagic fish enliven the blue depths. Proceeding toward the tip of the promontory, the wall

C - Images against the light. Here one can recognize whip corals, which are always very effective: the form of a diver in the distance gives the composition depth.

D - Butterflyfish (Chaetodon fasciatus) are common during dives as they swim alone near the gorgonians on whose polyps they feed.

becomes more vertical, embellished by luxuriant violet and red alcyonarians. One of the largest and densest gorgonian forests in the Red Sea can be found at a depth of 15 to 35 meters. The fans of these anthozoans may are two meters large, and are so close together that they create an extraordinary tangle of lacework. The gorgonians grow perpendicular to the walls, thus exposing as much area as possible to the current that brings in the plankton on which they feed.

G

E

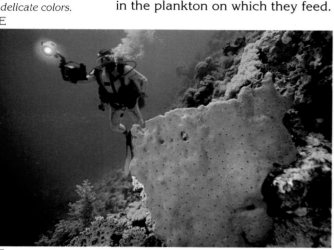

F

H

Many turkeyfish can be seen motionless among the branches as they lie in wait for the many anthias that swim close by. Especially sharp-eyed divers may spot pipefish, small gobies and hawkfish, expertly camouflaged by their reticulate color patterns among this tangle of gorgonians as they lie in wait for their prey. Looking out toward the open sea, you may spot large tunas, schools of jacks and sea breams passing by. Large masses of whip corals can be seen near the promontory, and just around the corner to the

north you will find a plateau known as "Fiasco", at depths varying from 7 to 25 meters, sloping gently downward. A school of fairly large barracudas can usually be seen swimming at the outer edge of the plateau, and is usually quite easy to approach.
Large groupers patrol this part of the reef, often accompanied by small whitetip sharks.
When the currents are strong, you may see eagle rays elegantly suspended at the water's surface.
Coral mushrooms rise from the floor, richly decorated by alcyonarians and red encrusting sponges, at the base of which are schools of batfish, some of which are being groomed by cleaner fish.

B

A

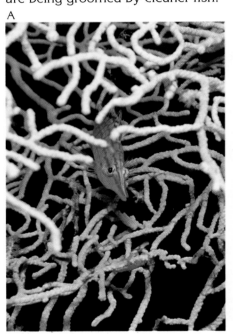

C

D

A - The hawkfish (Oxycirrhites typus) *is another predator that ambushes its victims by skillfully camouflaging itself among the branches of the gorgonians: if a shrimp or small fish unwisely comes too close, it darts out like an arrow, grabbing its victim with its strong beak.*

B - A group of batfish (Platax orbicularis) *moves slowly past the photographer. Batfish are not at all disturbed by divers, even when they come quite close. Due to their streamlined shape, these fish can remain immobile even against the current.*

C - During the day, turkeyfish (Pterois sp.) *prefer to take shelter among the branches of the gorgonians, where many of them may sometimes gather. They are not at all frightened of divers, who should nevertheless absolutely refrain from disturbing them.*

There are also emperors with absolutely no fear of the bubbles from divers' tanks. At shallower depths, you will swim among spectacular coral formations from the genera *Porites* and *Goniopora*. At Ras um Sid, after mooring your boat to a *shamandura*, use the line as a landmark for the descent, and once you have reached the desired depth, head for the point, keeping the wall to your left. During the first part of the dive, photographers can take lovely pictures by including the silhouette of the boats on the surface in the frame, with a colorful alcyonarian in the foreground. After you have reached the gorgonian forest, come up to a shallower depth, being careful not to go any deeper, as at certain times of the day there are strong currents running to the north, which may make it difficult or impossible to return to the boat. On your way back, stay deep enough to visit the glassfish cave. Your dive ends as you surface near the reef, where you can swim to the boat from the surface.
If the group is skilled enough, it is certainly more exciting to do Ras um Sid as a drift dive: the boat will drop you off at the cave, where you can descend diagonally, exploring the gorgonian area and then letting the current carry you.
After doubling the cape, you can surface along the Fiasco slope, where the boat will have followed your bubbles and be waiting to pick you up.
If you like underwater photography, you will certainly want to dive in this area more than once, first with a wide-angle lens for some seascape photos of gorgonians, and then with other lenses to pick out the colorful inhabitants of the reef.
If you prefer macrophotography, you will have so many subjects that you'll run out of film before you know it.
Ras um Sid is a dive for everyone, and only during drift dives will you need to be experienced.

E

F

G

H

D - *Their natural curiosity leads the peaceful humphead wrasse (Cheilinus undulatus) to approach divers and follow them for part of their dive. The humphead wrasse is a common sight along Red Sea reefs, but in these waters they are exceptionally large.*

E - *A tiny blenny (Ecsenius nalolo), about 5-6 centimeters in size, peers from its hiding place at an even smaller reef inhabitant: a goby. These curious situations are frequent, but few divers ever see them, because, unfortunately, most of them do not know how to examine the reef carefully.*

F - *A school of fusiliers (Caesio sp.) moves rapidly past the divers. When these fish gather in very compact groups, it is difficult for predators to tell them apart and thus make a successful attack.*

G - *A group of barracudas (Sphyraena qenie) comes in from the open sea to patrol their territory. These formidable predators, who are completely harmless to divers, move in groups that may consist of hundreds of individuals.*

H - *When in areas that push out into the open sea, it is always a good idea to look out to the blue depths from time to time, where you may see pelagic fish passing by. In this photograph, a pair of eagle rays (Aetobatus narinari) glide elegantly past the photographer.*

TEMPLE

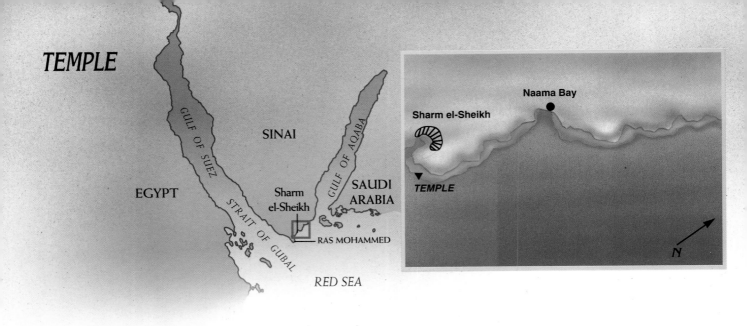

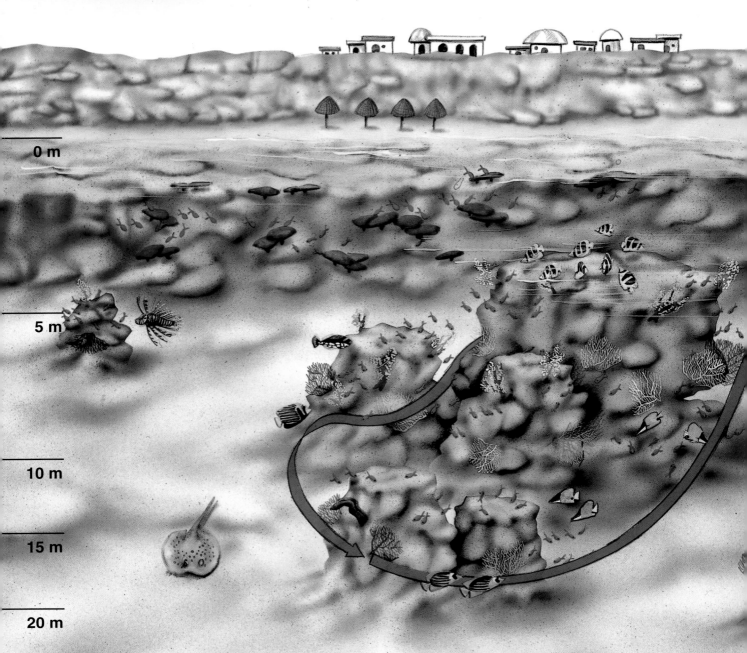

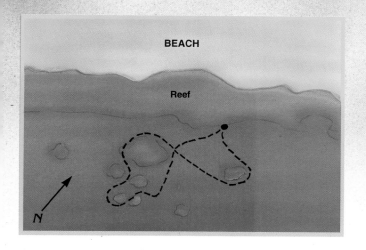

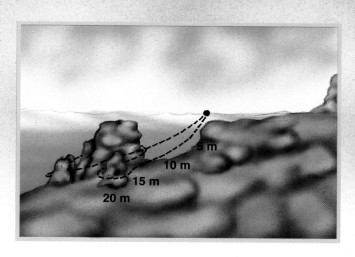

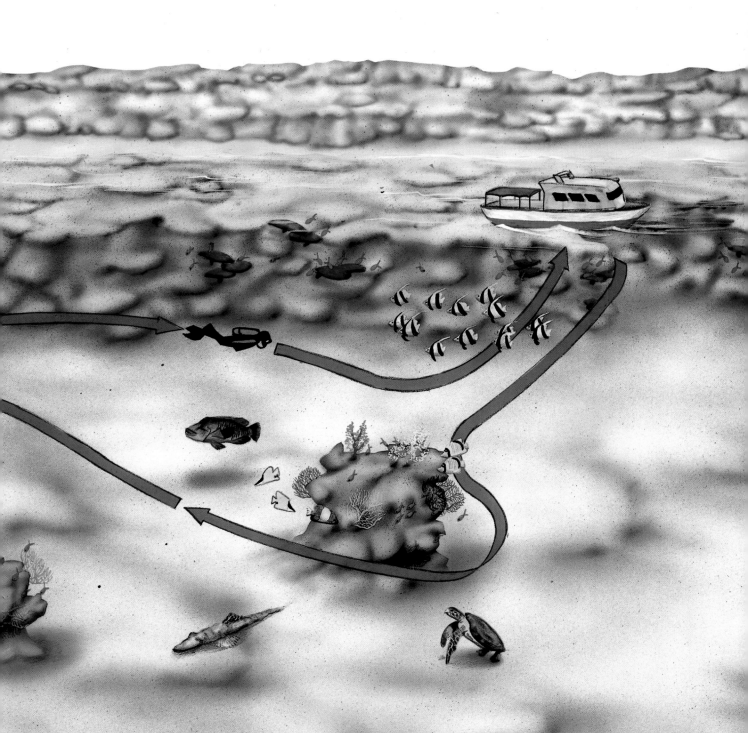

A

B

C

Temple is one of the most popular areas with scuba divers staying at Sharm el-Sheikh. Usually the first check dives take place here, and near the shore there is a natural swimming pool with a floor of white sand, ideal for first-time forays in open water diving courses. Temple is also perfect for night dives because of its shallowness and the luxuriant life on its coral mushrooms. Heading north from the bay of Sharm el-Maya, you'll reach Temple in a little over 10 minutes. Numerous mooring lines are set in the center of the gulf, where there is a beach with a vacation village. It borders Ras um Sid to the north and Ras Katy to the south.

D

A - This rare image shows three crocodile fish (Cociella crocodila) lined up next to each other, probably for reproductive purposes.

B - As you explore around the coral towers at Temple, you can see the reef inhabitants intent on their normal activities, not disturbed in the slightest by the presence of divers. A turkeyfish (Pterois sp.) stalks a small fish among the alcyonarians, its pectoral fins open to force the fish into an area which will cut off its escape.

C - This photograph shows the dense network on the snout of the humphead wrasse (Cheilinus undulatus). The bump on the front of its head is present in older, larger individuals.

D - Corals have colonized the upper portions of all the protuberances on the sea floor, in spectacular, bizarre forms.

The reef, which is not far from the shore, drops vertically to the sand at a depth of 4-6 meters, and the floor descends gently to a depth of 20-25 meters and then plunges off into the abyss. The bathymetric depth of 10 to 20 meters from the sea bottom contains numerous coral pinnacles that form a sort of colonnade, thus giving the area its name. There are about ten towers, some of which rise to just a few meters from the surface, and the largest one almost rises above it. Even snorkelers can explore it easily. Despite the large number of divers in this area, the corals are still in good condition due to the professionalism of the dive guides, who are quite careful about

E

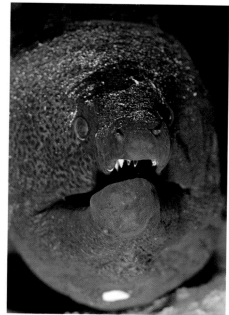

by its powerful upper jaw out of line with the lower jaw, thus giving it a very ugly expression. Encounters with turtles and humphead wrasses are quite common, and they will confidently approach divers. Blue-spotted stingrays lie in sandy and detrital areas, along with crocodile fish which are well-camouflaged against the sea bed. Triggerfish, their heads down, stir up the floor by blowing jets of water from their mouths as they search for food. A word of advice on triggerfish: during certain periods, usually around the full moon, they may become aggressive enough to bite anyone who approaches their egg-filled nests (recognizable as bowl-shaped depressions in the sandy

be used for seascapes and macros which are not too extreme. This is one of the most beautiful areas for night dives. By night, Temple always provides interesting encounters. The alcyonarians are populated by small crustaceans, while parrotfish take shelter in the crevices, covering themselves with mucus as protection against nocturnal predators. It is not uncommon to see the queen of the night: the Spanish dancer, a large, beautiful nudibranch which will shine bright red in your flashlight beam. For macro photos, the *Nikonos* and extension rings will provide excellent results, especially if you use the dual camera-flash in TTL mode.

F

G

environmental protection. Brightly colored alcyonarians ranging from deep violet to yellow are attached to the walls of the pinnacles, around which swim clouds of red anthias. At the base of the coral formations grow large gorgonian fans which sometimes obstruct the passage from one column to another. Pairs of masked butterflyfish share the shade of the crevices with bright yellow grunts with black spots, and there are always emperors swimming about. The small saddle which has developed between the largest tower and the rocky formation that seems cut by the large pinnacle is home to a large moray which has become a mascot for divers. It is easily recognizable

floor). After mooring the boat to one of the *shamandura*, or mooring lines, in the area, descend along the line and begin your dive at the bottom. The area is not very large, and you'll move around coral formations that change in circumference as you descend. End your dive by coming back up the mooring line, so that you'll have a clear landmark for your safety stop at 5 meters deep. I advise underwater photographers to use cameras with lenses such as the 28 or 35 mm, to pick out small groups of fish or individual specimens. If you have a reflex camera with an underwater case, the ideal lens is a 28-70 zoom, which is quite versatile and can

E - The lair of this gigantic moray (Gymnothorax javanicus), which has become the mascot for Sharm el-Sheikh dive guides, is at the central tower at Temple. During the day, the moray peeps out of its lair, poking part of its body out and curiously watching the scene before it.

F - Avoiding abrupt movements, a diver approaches a turtle intent on searching for food on the reef. A family of turtles lives near the pinnacles, where it can be seen even during night dives.

G - A group of yellow-spotted grunts (Plectorhynchus gaterinus) meets a diver. Using special techniques, you can approach fish without frightening them.

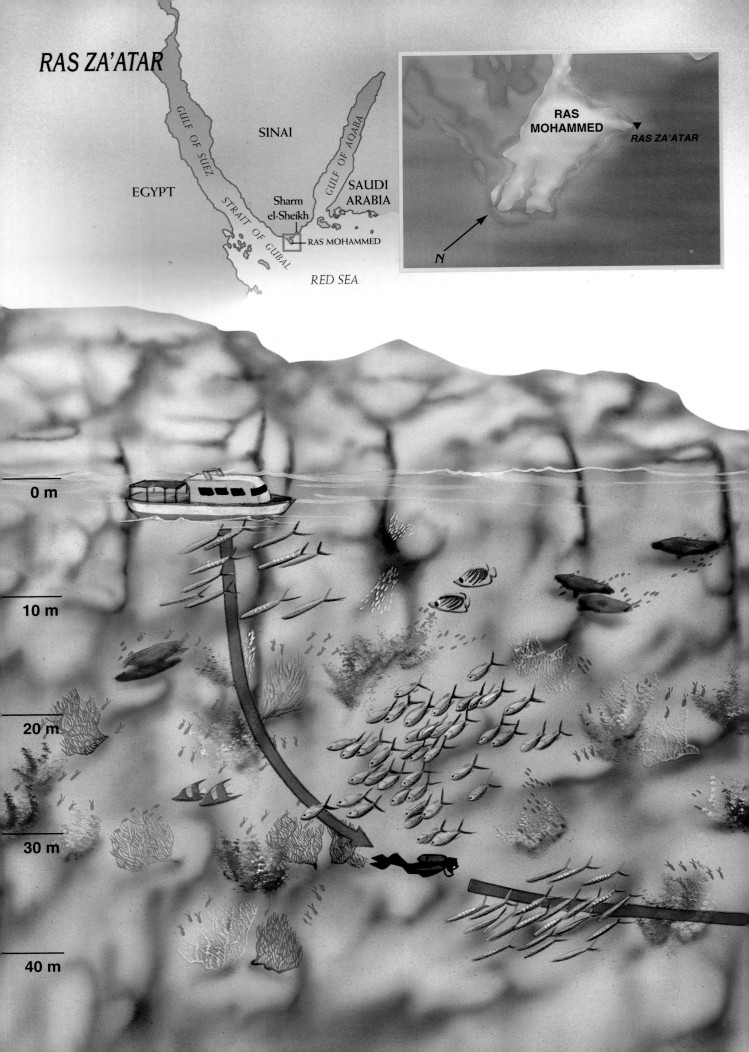

RAS ZA'ATAR

SINAI

GULF OF SUEZ

GULF OF AQABA

EGYPT

STRAIT OF GUBAL

SAUDI ARABIA

Sharm el-Sheikh

RAS MOHAMMED

RED SEA

RAS MOHAMMED

RAS ZA'ATAR

N

0 m

10 m

20 m

30 m

40 m

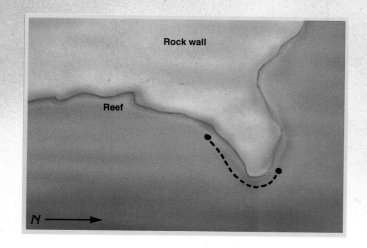

Rock wall

Reef

N →

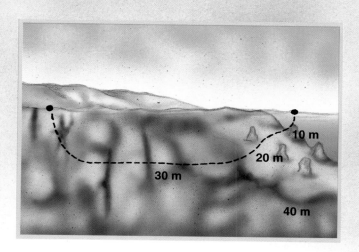

10 m

20 m

30 m

40 m

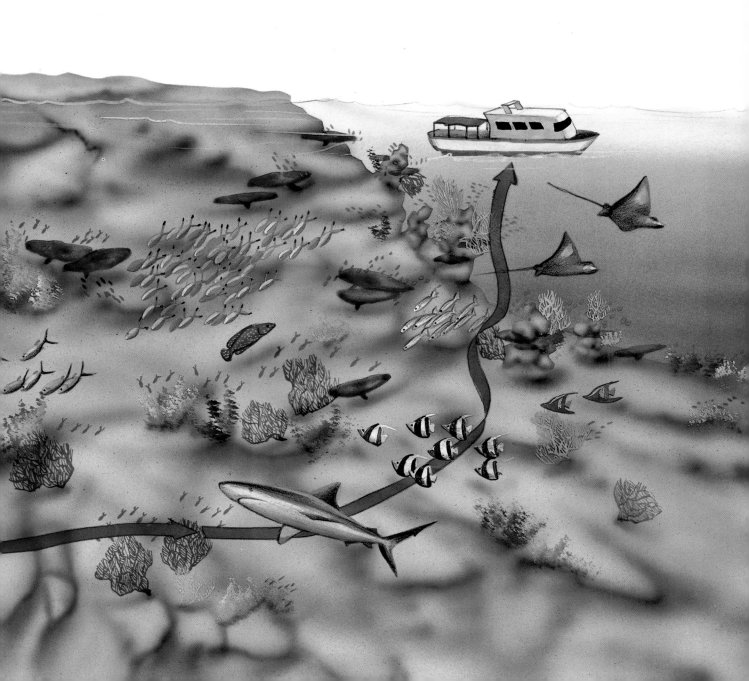

Za'atar is about a forty minute sail south of Sharm el-Maya. More precisely, it is the cape that borders the deep Marsa Bareika inlet to the south. It is in the Ras Mohammed marine park district, and for purposes of environmental protection the northern portion of Marsa Bareika is closed to diving, while two permanent mooring lines are located in the more internal southern portion. When the sea is rough and the wind is blowing from the south, these lines offer a peaceful mooring place and can be the starting point for an entertaining alternative dive especially suitable for beginners.

A - A solitary jackfish patrols the wall in search of an easy prey. You should stay at about 20 meters deep during this dive, where the sun illuminates the wall and creates fascinating plays of light.

B - Clusters of alcyonarians take on particular shades of color and stand out from the reef in all their beauty. Clouds of anthias move jerkily, following the rhythmic pulse of the coral reef.

C - When you dive in these waters so full of marine fauna, you should interrupt your exploration of the wall from time to time and look out to the open sea: as the area is sometimes swept by powerful currents and is patrolled by large jackfish, you will probably not be disappointed.

It is not possible to anchor around Ras Za'atar, and thus a drift dive is necessary. As the wall descends vertically from the surface to the abyss and there are sometimes powerful currents, only divers with good basic skills should attempt the descent. Enter the water about a hundred meters south of the cape, and once you have reached the desired depth, proceed northward, keeping the wall to your left. At about 30 meters deep, the wall opens into several deep caves, around the entrances to which grow large black coral trees and gorgonians. You should carry an underwater flashlight so you can see the large groupers that make their lairs in the less illuminated areas of the crevices and are usually surrounded by numerous cleaner fish. Using due caution, it is possible to come quite close to these members of the *Serranidae* family. Even at shallower depths, there are numerous cracks where various types of groupers and morays coexist. Of particular beauty is a vertical crack in the reef that reaches the surface. In it swim compact, dense schools of glassfish that reflect the silvery rays of the sun filtering in from above. The wall is quite irregular, with spurs of rock that jut out to the open sea, alternating with deep cracks.

Bushes of black coral and colorful gorgonians of all sizes can seen everywhere. As you near the point, the sights become even more spectacular. Pink, lilac, red and other colored alcyonarians are particularly dense in this area, and clouds of orange and violet anthias move jerkily near the corals. The background is a deep sea blue. Places like these have given the Red Sea its reputation as the most colorful sea in the world. Before doubling the cape and entering Marsa Bareika, you should spend some time looking out to the open sea. Large jackfish patrol the outer reef, and it is not uncommon to see record sized specimens.

In the early morning you are likely to see eagle rays moving effortlessly against the current and flying elegantly near the water's surface. *Plectopromus* groupers, abandoning their lairs, lie in wait near the surface, on the lookout for schools of fusiliers. The unmistakable outline of sharks can be seen in the deeper blue waters. Right around the corner, the wall descends more gently, with several coral pinnacles rising from the sea floor at a depth of 10 meters. Above one of these towers a formation of black coral, an ochre colored gorgonian, a blue one, and several yellow alcyonarians grow together, providing an unforgettable shot for underwater photographers with a wide-angle lens. The boat will pick up divers about 20 meters within the Gulf of Bareika, near the wall where you will have passed your last few minutes for decompression. Underwater cameras provide excellent results when 16 or 18 mm underwater lenses are used, or with a 15 mm lens on an amphibious camera. Don't forget the 28 mm lens for pelagic fish swimming in the open sea.

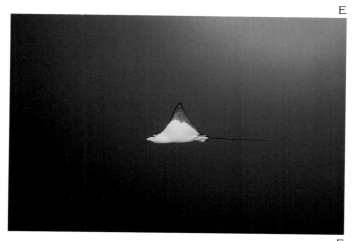

E

F

G

D - The wall at Ras Za'atar is full of delicately-branched gorgonians. These rich waters have permitted the extraordinary development of all species of corals, especially alcyonarians and gorgonians.

E - The silhouette of an elegant eagle ray (Aetobatus narinari) interrupts the infinite blue depths around Ras Za'atar.

F - Sharks are at the top of the reef food chain. Usually active predators, in some cases they perform the vital role of "garbage collectors," feeding on dead animals or preying on weaker and sick animals, thus guaranteeing the natural selection of the other species.

G - This photograph shows the branches of a gorgonian. The polyps expanded to capture food carried in by the current only increase its gracefulness.

JACKFISH ALLEY

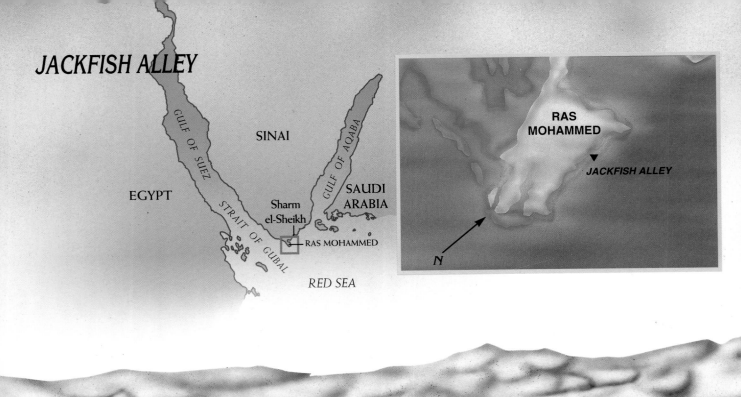

SINAI

GULF OF SUEZ

GULF OF AQABA

EGYPT

STRAIT OF GUBAL

Sharm el-Sheikh

SAUDI ARABIA

RAS MOHAMMED

RED SEA

RAS MOHAMMED

JACKFISH ALLEY

N

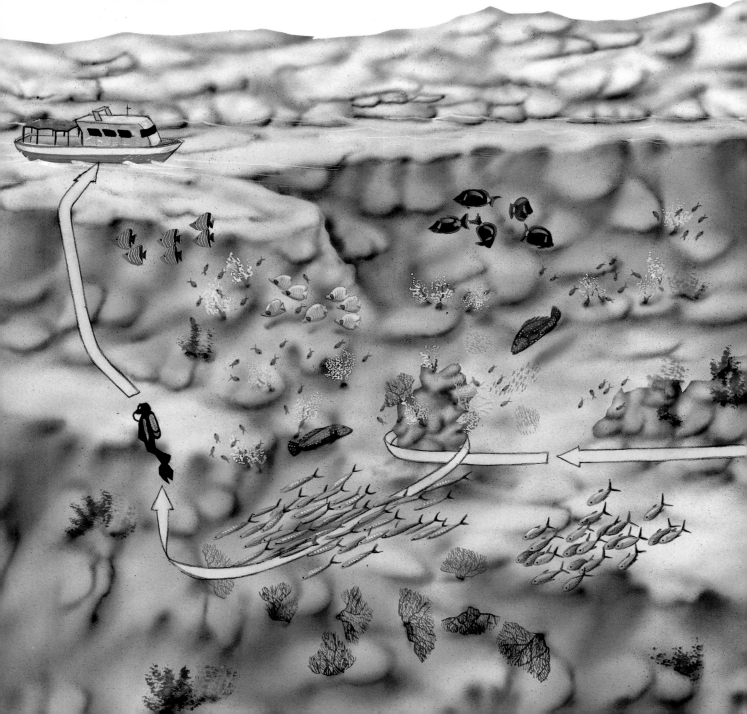

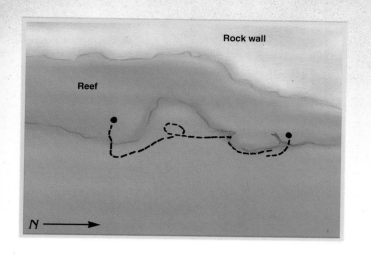

Reef

Rock wall

N →

5 m

10 m

15 m

20 m

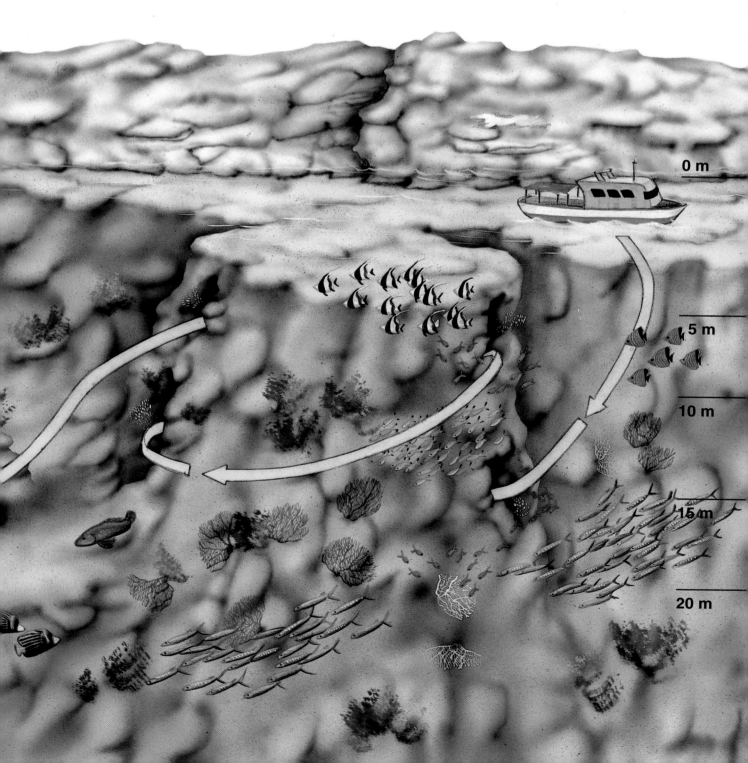

0 m

5 m

10 m

15 m

20 m

This diving area, also known as "Fisherman's Bank", is located along the reef that runs from Ras Za'atar at the sea's edge to Ras Mohammed. About an hour's sail from Sharm el-Maya, you will reach a point which is easily identifiable by the white spot on the vertical wall of the reef. There are no permanent mooring lines, so a drift dive is necessary. Dive only when the sea is calm, as the dive includes shallow caves where the surf can be rough. Under normal conditions, this dive is appropriate for all skill levels, and for many divers Jackfish Alley is their first experience of diving in caves. As it is less than 20 meters deep, it can be an afternoon dive or

B

A

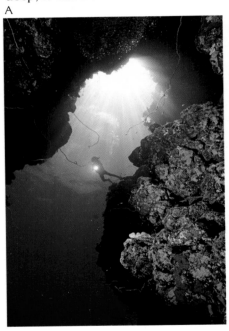

C

the third dive of the day. The boat will drop you off near the reef, right under the white spot. At this point, the wall descends vertically, and you will see the entrance to the first group of caves at a depth of 5 meters. I recommend not entering right away, but descending to 8 meters, keeping the wall to the right and moving a little south, until you see another large opening which connects to the first one. Here you will enter a large chamber, with a dark area to the left, which will require an underwater flashlight to explore. To the right, a crack allows the light to enter from above, filtering in through dense swarms of glassfish that reflect it in silvery flashes. Large spotted groupers can usually be seen sheltered behind some protuberance as cleaner fish free them of parasites. Going forward a few meters, the cave branches off: to the left is a wide area with a white sandy bottom, illuminated by a shaft of light that enters from a small crack in the upper reef. Groups of golden glassfish are inundated by this light, creating a truly magical effect. Taking the right branch and rising up a couple of meters, you will come out onto the outside wall. Continue your dive by keeping the reef to the right and descending diagonally to a depth of 14 meters, where there is a sandy plateau. Near a rocky formation detached from the wall is a second group of caves. Here as well, the entry is quite

A - During certain hours of the day, the sunlight filtering down from above creates beautiful plays of light and shadow. From inside the caves, you can take very effective photos that clearly show the conformation of the caverns.

B - Caves are common in this diving area. The large caverns provide a pleasant underwater exploration even for divers who are not comfortable in caves.

C - In the more sheltered and less illuminated areas of the cracks, there are large spotted groupers which reach over one meter in length. If you move cautiously, you can approach these splendid predators and examine them close up.

D

E

D, E - Glassfish are typical cave inhabitants. Here, both species are present. The first is Pempheris vanicolensis, *a bronze-colored fish which is somewhat hatchet-shaped. The second,* Parapriacanthus guentheri, *is a small fish which rarely reaches eight centimeters in size. The front part of its body is pink and the back portion is almost transparent, and it has bioluminescent organs that make it shine even when it's not illuminated by a flashlight beam.*

*F - This close-up of a turkeyfish (*Pterois sp.*) shows the conformation of its head, adorned with the antennae and barbels typical of this sedentary but effective predator.*

G - Cave floors are usually sedimentary, so you must watch your position to avoid raising particles which would cloud the water and reduce visibility.

*H - Bigeye trevallies (*Caranx sexfasciatus*) make rapid incursions into the caves, which have various exits, in an attempt to isolate and attack a glassfish.*

I - Near the caves is a true explosion of life and color, and underwater photographers usually end their dives around these extraordinary and colorful alcyonarians.

wide and the crack rises to 4 meters from the surface. Looking upward, you will see a truly amazing sight: thousands of glassfish moving in unison from one side of the cave to the other, creating extraordinary plays of light. A wide-angle lens is indispensable for good underwater shots, and the depth of the surroundings can only be captured by snapping a good portion of the caves from close range. Lovely photos can be taken against the light from within a cave, with a cloud of glassfish in the foreground. These fish reflect a great deal of light, so use the flash sparingly. When you have left the second cave, stay at a depth of about 15 meters and, once you have crossed the sandy plateau

F

going south, you will see a coral mushroom richly adorned with red and purple alcyonarians, around which swim more small glassfish. There are often many surgeonfish hovering near the surface. Leaving the pinnacle, which will certainly provide other photo opportunities, move south along a sort of sandy road. When there is a slight current, you will see small whitetip sharks lying here. Encounters with groups of barracudas and jacks are also common here. You will emerge some distance from the shore, so you should send an inflatable signal buoy to the surface while you complete your usual safety decompression. The support boat will then approach to pick you up.

G

H

I

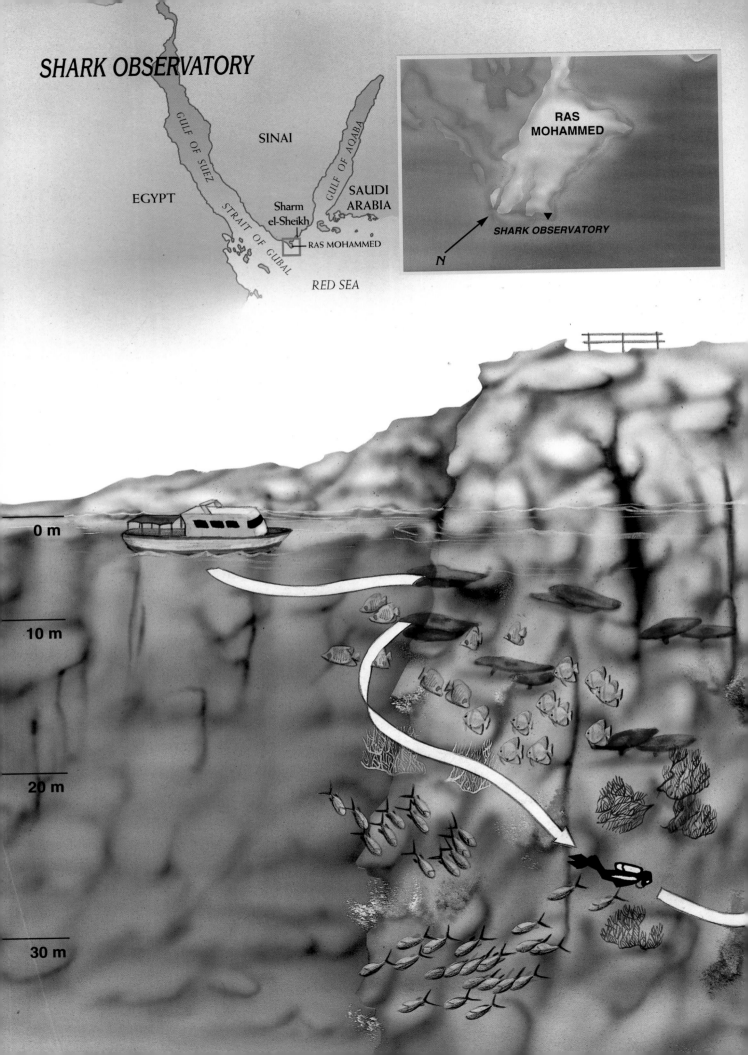

SHARK OBSERVATORY

GULF OF SUEZ
STRAIT OF GUBAL
GULF OF AQABA
SINAI
EGYPT
SAUDI ARABIA
Sharm el-Sheikh
RAS MOHAMMED
RED SEA

RAS MOHAMMED
SHARK OBSERVATORY
N

0 m
10 m
20 m
30 m

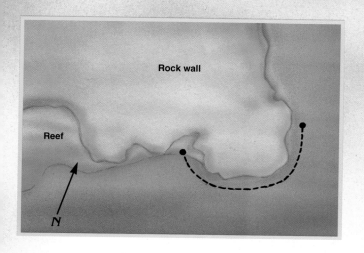

Rock wall

Reef

N

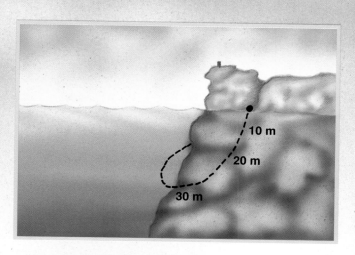

10 m

20 m

30 m

A

B

C

From the port of Sharm el-Maya, head south, and in about 40 minutes you'll see a high reef, the southern side of which, when seen from a certain angle and using a bit of imagination, resembles the profile of a head: Ras Mohammed, the Prophet's Head. On top of the rocky spur is a lookout which was once used to observe the sharks which used to frequent the shallow waters of the cape in great numbers. Today this sight has become more rare, but the view from the top of Shark Observatory is still extraordinary. Your excursion will explore the submerged part of this mountain, starting from the northwest side,

D

which has more marine life, and proceeding south, keeping the wall to your right. There are no permanent mooring lines, so you must use drift dive techniques. The reef plunges into the sea, and after a narrow fringe of surface coral it descends down almost vertically: the term "wall dive" really means something here.
Down to 10-12 meters, the coral wall is punctured by little caves and crevices, within which are shiny masses of glassfish.
You should use an underwater flashlight to explore the dark parts of these cavities, which are home to redmouth groupers and soldierfish who only leave

A - The high buttresses of Shark Observatory rise from the waters of the Ras Mohammed promontory. The wall continues underwater in a vertical drop down to the abyss.

B - A whitetip shark (Triaenodon obesus) swims peacefully in the deeper part of the reef.

C - The walls that plunge down into the intense blue of the depths are completely carpeted by alcyonarians in a thousand colors. Walls like this have given the Red Sea its well-deserved fame as the most colorful sea in the world.

D - Whip corals growing toward the light rise up from the wall. These colonies grow rather rapidly and are little affected by predators.

E - There are roofed coral formations in the shallower part of the reef that form natural shelters for various species of fish, in this case a swarm of glassfish, which reflects silvery flashes of light in the beam of the flashlight.

F - Two divers, keeping a perfectly neutral position, admire the frenetic activity of a group of anthias.

G - These gorgonians look like a mouth with a turkeyfish resting inside.

H - A group of black-spotted grunts (Plectorhynchus gaterinus) hovers in the shelter of a big Acropora formation.

I - A compact formation of elegant batfish with their unmistakable flat bodies poses for the photographer.

E

sizes and colors grow luxuriantly, forming a sort of cascade of soft bushes. If you look closely, you can see their expanded polyps like the corollas of flowers, opening and closing incessantly to capture the plankton on which they feed. Red and orange anthias move rhythmically, as if in time with the breath of the reef, moving back and forth from the wall as they follow mysterious impulses. You are at the southern tip of the Sinai Peninsula, and in these waters encounters with pelagic fish are commonplace. Large jackfish, tunas and sharks are frequent sights if you don't allow yourself to be overly distracted by the beauty of the

wall and are careful to look out to sea often. At the end of the dive, after your safety stop at a depth of 5 meters, you'll come to the surface near the reef, where you can reach the boat by swimming from the surface. When you dive at Shark Observatory you'll feel as if you were suspended over a bottomless abyss, so you will need to constantly check your underwater computer to avoid being lured by the fascination of the deep sea and going beyond the safe limits for recreational diving. There are many subjects to photograph, so your choice of lenses will be merely a question of personal taste.

F

G

the shadow of their lairs at night. The whole reef is broken by vertical cracks similar to small canyons, with walls that are often embellished by red encrusting sponges and groups of beautiful little fluorescent purple dottybacks, who dart from their territory rapidly only to capture some of the zooplankton carried in by the current. Large gorgonians grow everywhere on the wall, with fans that undulate perpendicular to the flow of the current. If you look carefully, you can see the little inhabitants that find shelter among the dense horny network, including gobies, pipefish and crabs. Alcyonarians in various

H

I

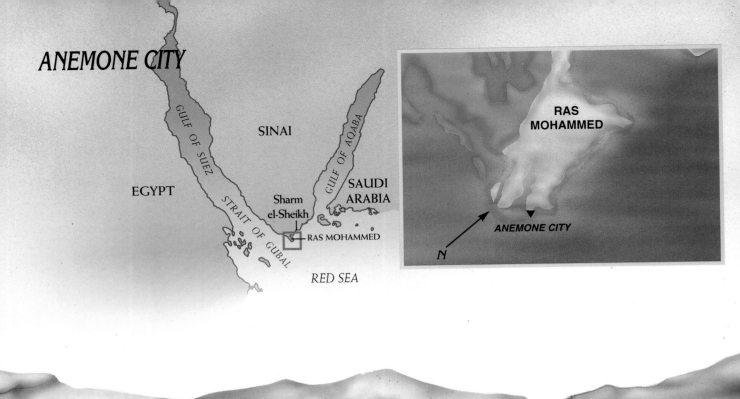

ANEMONE CITY

GULF OF SUEZ

SINAI

GULF OF AQABA

EGYPT

STRAIT OF GUBAL

Sharm
el-Sheikh

SAUDI
ARABIA

RAS MOHAMMED

RED SEA

RAS
MOHAMMED

ANEMONE CITY

N

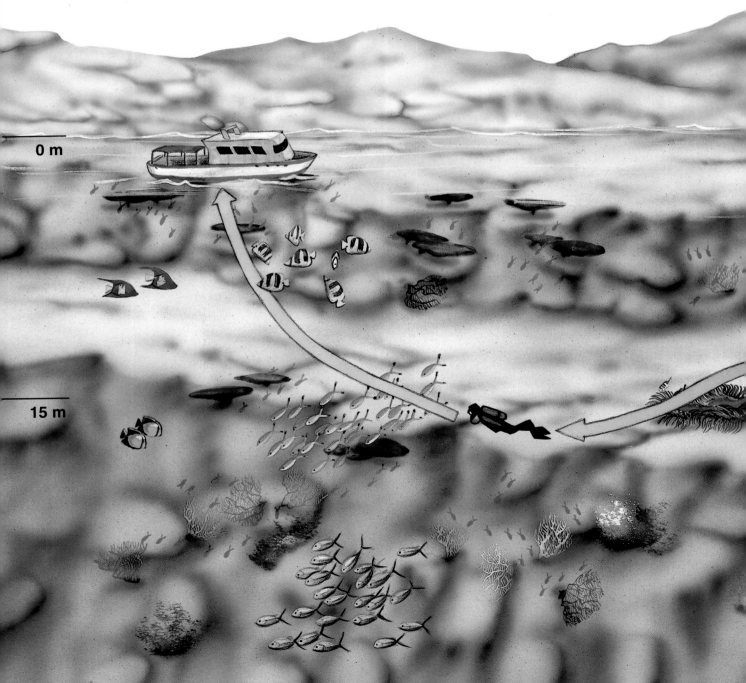

0 m

15 m

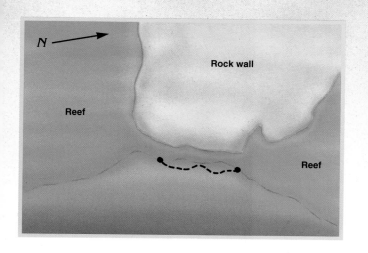

N

Rock wall

Reef

Reef

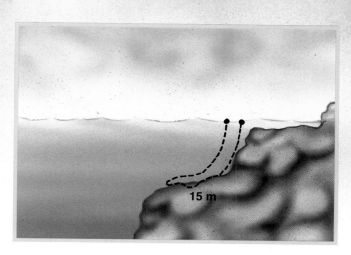

15 m

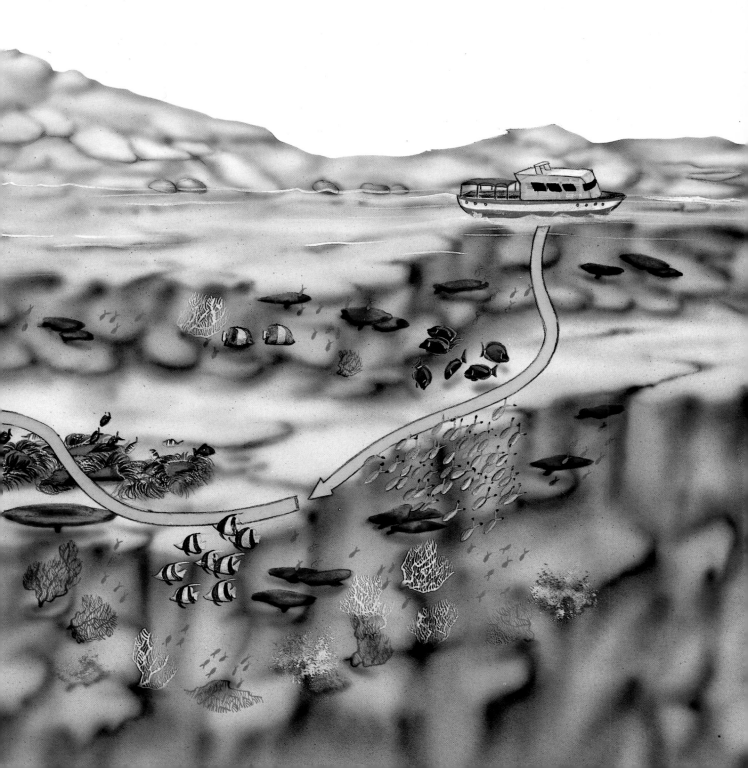

Anemone City is a little less than an hour's sail from Sharm el-Maya, heading south to the southernmost part of the Sinai. After reaching Shark Observatory, which is recognizable by the lookout that provides a breathtaking view, head toward the semi-emerged platform of Shark Reef. At a depth of between 15 and 20 meters, not far from this coral formation broken off from the reef, the wall, which descends vertically, forms a sort of terrace that juts out into the open sea. The dive begins from this platform. The Anemone City plateau gets its name from the dozens of *Heteractis magnifica* anemones that cover it. The disks of these anthozoans, which can reach one meter in diameter and are almost attached to each other, are home to dozens of clown anemonefish, which move ceaselessly, reminding one of the frenetic activity of a modern city. Any dive along the southern coast of the Sinai will turn up numerous anemones, but nowhere else are they as concentrated as they are here. This may be due to the existence of a thermal spring that creates ideal conditions for the development of the anemones. Two species of fish live in symbiosis with them: clown anemonefish and domino damselfish. The first is a beautiful orange color with a darker dorsal area and two blue-white vertical bands on each side of the body. Usually only one pair of clown anemonefish colonize the anemone, but here the tangle of tentacles is so vast that dozens of fish live together. Clown anemonefish spend their lives in symbiosis with the anemone that acts as their host. The female in the group is the largest, and if she dies, the largest male takes her place by becoming female. These highly territorial fish (they do not hesitate to attack divers if they come too close to their territory) are immune to the stinging substances of the anemone's tentacles, and when in danger they take refuge among the branches of their host. The other common inhabitant of the carpet of anemones is the domino damselfish, a small, almost black fish with a small white spot on the flanks.

A

B

C

Young individuals also have a white spot above the eyes. Domino damselfish live in symbiosis with the anemones until they are adults, and then they abandon them to live in groups of about a dozen individuals, with a dominant male and many females. Photographers can use a wide-angle lens to capture the expanse of anemones, perhaps with a diver in the background. A 28 mm lens will be useful to pick out groups of small fish, being careful to shoot from below to highlight the perspective. While snapping your pictures, be careful not to touch the reef and damage the corals. On the plateau, and in particular on the outer edge, are vast formations of umbrella corals, around which there

A - The concentration of anemones in this area is truly exceptional. If you explore the sea bottom, you will see dozens of anemones, one attached to the other, undulating to the rhythm of the sea. Clown anemonefish (Amphiprion bicinctus) and domino damselfish (Dascillus trimaculatus) live symbiotically with the anemones, the former passing their entire lives among the tentacles of their host, and the latter taking refuge among the anemones only when juveniles.

B - The relationship between anemonefish, which may reach twelve centimeters in length, and sea anemones is a typical example of mutualism.

C - The schools of fusiliers (Caesio sp.) are sometimes so dense that they block the sunlight. A compact school is the only form of defense for many species, who would otherwise be left totally helpless against predators.

D - A clown anemonefish (Amphiprion bicinctus) peeps out warily from the tentacles of its anemone, which in this case is a splendid Heteractis aurora. These fish are very territorial and will not hesitate to attack divers who come too close.

D

E

F

are always some spotted angelfish. The fans of the gorgonians grow on the walls. The area is frequented by schools of metallic blue fusiliers, the prey of the jacks lying in wait for them. As Anemone City is in the southernmost part of the Red Sea, spectacular encounters are always possible. During our last dive, we were approached by a shovel-nosed ray who followed us for several minutes. Anemone City is the usual point of departure for a dive that, depending on the current, can proceed toward the gorge and the plateau between Shark Reef and the coast, or else north toward the wall of Shark Observatory. In either case it is a dive where the boat is in motion, and should thus be planned carefully.

G

E - This photograph shows the mouth of an anemone, in this case a Heteractis magnifica. Anemonefish can live among the stinging tentacles by covering their bodies with mucus. The anemone recognizes the mucus of its anemonefish and avoids striking it with its stinging cells.

F - This coral umbrella populated by dozens of brightly colored fish, is another example of how constructor corals build structures in an enormous variety of shapes and sizes.

G - There are imposing Acropora formations on the outer edge of the plateau of Anemone City.

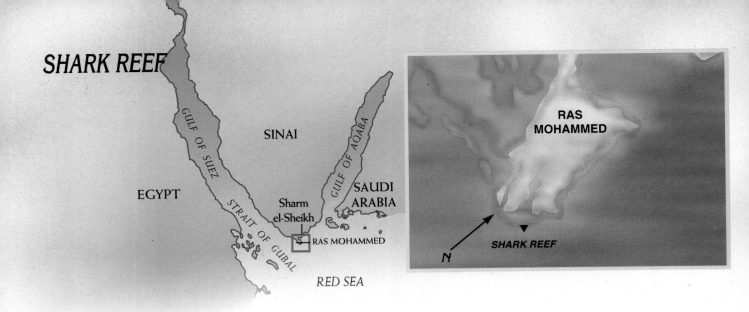

SHARK REEF

GULF OF SUEZ

SINAI

GULF OF AQABA

STRAIT OF GUBAL

EGYPT

Sharm
el-Sheikh

SAUDI
ARABIA

RAS MOHAMMED

RED SEA

RAS
MOHAMMED

SHARK REEF

N

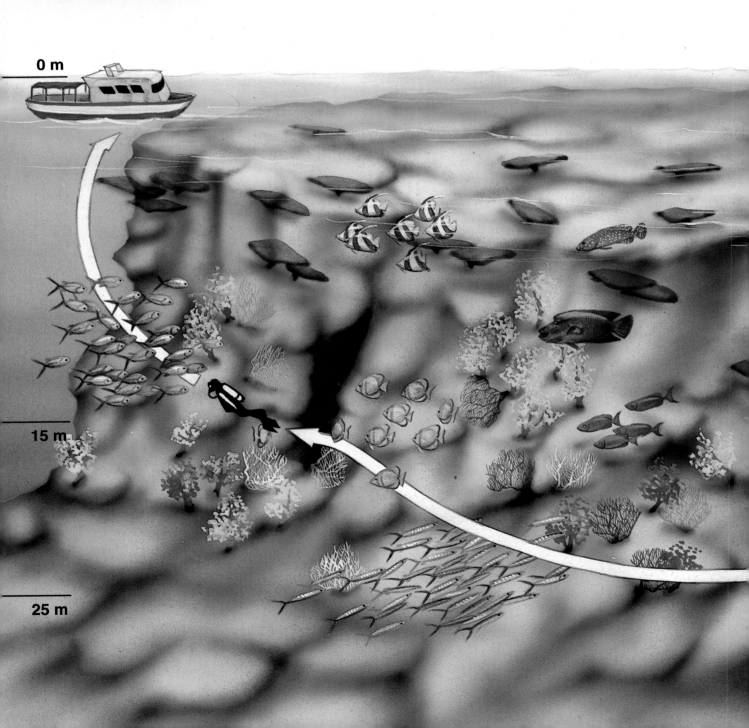

0 m

15 m

25 m

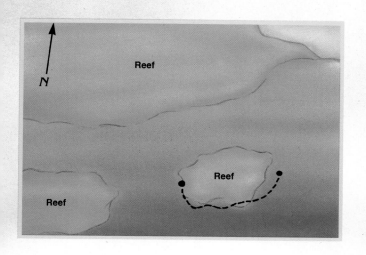

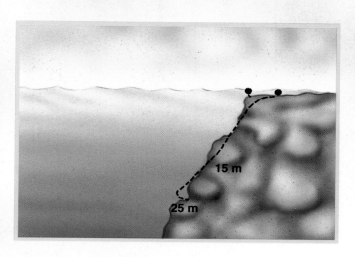

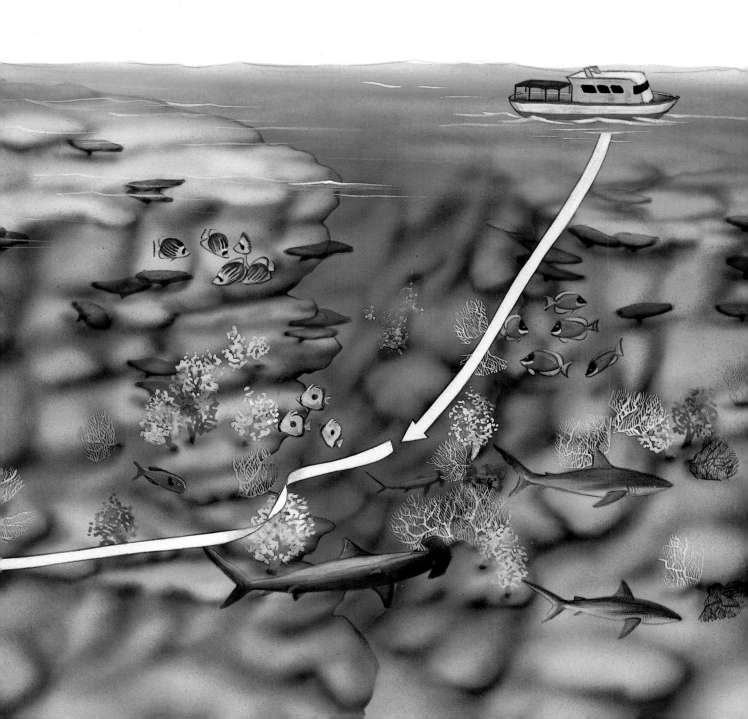

This is beyond doubt the most famous area in the entire Red Sea. To be exact, it is the first of the two semi-emerged reefs located about 40 minutes south of Sharm el-Maya, at the southern tip of the Ras Mohammed district. The Sinai Peninsula, wedged into the Red Sea between Arabia and Egypt, ends to the south in a long lagoon bordering on the emerged reef. Outside the lagoon is a valley between 10 and 15 meters deep, with a mixed sand and coral bottom, that then rises to the surface in two large coral towers, Jolanda and Shark Reef, which are about 50 meters apart. Beyond them the reef plunges vertically to a bathymetric depth

B

D

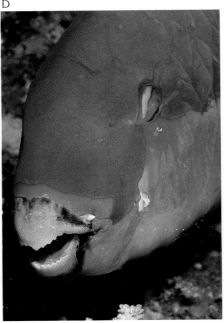

C

of about 800 meters. The outside wall of Shark Reef is incessantly swept by currents which carry in plankton and other nourishment, thus attracting huge numbers of fish and their natural predators to this area. The constantly moving waters create ideal conditions for the growth of soft and hard corals, and the concentration and size of these anthozoans are truly remarkable. This combination of factors creates extraordinary biodiversity, and Shark Reef is considered one of the most beautiful dives in the world: many divers say it is the most beautiful anywhere. After exploring around this coral tower, it would be easier to name the creatures that you didn't see, as the list of fish and corals you can admire here is endless. You can moor the boat to a permanent *shamandura*, but you should only do so when there is no current. Usually a drift dive is preferable, starting from the east side of Shark Reef and watching the intensity of the current, which meets the reef at this point and separates into two flows, one heading toward the saddle between the reef and the coast, and the other out to the open sea. Another option could be to dive in at Anemone City and, keeping the wall to your right, descend to a depth of about 20 meters, where the current is less powerful, and reach your destination without

F

G

E

tiring yourself out. You can also do this dive from land, starting at Hidden Bay, but this is highly inadvisable due to the possible rough currents that could prevent you from returning to the beach when your dive is over. Proceed clockwise, and enormous gorgonians will appear on the wall, with lacework that shelters tiny gobies and numerous hawkfish. If you look more closely you will see small, rare, brightly-colored crustaceans. Enormous isolated reddish-pink alcyonarians grow on the protuberances of the reef and become extremely dense where the current directly hits the wall. You can see the expanded polyps on these soft, bush-like corals as

A - Large soft corals have colonized the protruding areas of the reef.

B - Surgeonfish (Naso hexacanthus) gather to hover in the blue depths near the vertical walls. These fish follow the flow of zooplankton on which they feed. They are not shy, and divers find it easy to approach them.

C - During the winter months, gray sharks (Carcharhinus amblyrhynchos) - here one specimen is behind a school of grunts (Plectorhynchus gaterinus) - following the reproductive urge, go to shallow waters near the saddle between Shark Reef and Jolanda Reef, where you can watch their courting rituals.

D - This close-up of a male parrotfish (Scarus gibbus) shows the sturdy teeth this fish uses to break off corals to carry away the algae that is part of its normal diet.

E - Alcyonarians have grown so luxuriantly on the walls of Shark Reef that the reef seems lined with a thick carpet in a thousand colors.

F - Large humphead wrasses (Cheilinus undulatus) may follow divers for some distance. This one is accompanied by a jackfish, who uses its companion's bulk to approach its prey unseen.

G - The fans of the gorgonians with their delicate networks are home to a myriad of small animals which often escape an inattentive eye. They are only a few centimeters long, but have incredible shapes and colors.

A - Jackfish
(Caranx sp.) are
also permanent
guests in the area.
Sometimes divers
will have a chance
to watch these
swift predators
as they hunt:
they dart forward
in unison like
silvery arrows,
using special
strategies to drive
into the schools
of small fish.

B - Sheltered
on the southern
part of the reef are
large barracudas
(Sphyraena sp.),
which when the
current is weak
will usually circle
about in groups
of about a dozen
individuals.

C - The deeper
waters are the
realm of
hammerhead
sharks (Sphyrna
lewini), the lords
of the sea, who
can be seen in
groups in the
early morning
as they follow
their migratory
routes, paying
absolutely no
attention to divers.

D - Any kind
of encounter is
possible at Shark
Reef. Due to its
particular
geographical
position in an area
where currents
carry in
nourishment,
every link in
the food chain
is represented.

A

B

C

D

they take in nourishment, looking
for all the world like a big flower
garden just spattered with snow.
Everything around you stands out
against the deep blue sea, and the
red forms of the anthias create
a uniquely beautiful atmosphere.
During some periods of the year
enormous groups of red breams
gather here, forming a living wall
that runs from the surface to great
depths. Nowhere else in the world
can you see anything like this, and
words cannot describe how you
will feel as you cross this sparkling
pink mass. Once you make your
way through the wall of breams,
you'll come to another
breathtaking sight: a large school
of big barracudas hovering near
the surface, forming a
continuously moving silver ball.
Under these extraordinary masses
of fish you'll see the forms of the
lords of the sea: hammerhead
sharks, who patrol the deeper
areas of the reef by brushing the
water with their long tails.
Your ever-present diving
companions will be humphead
wrasses, who will curiously come
so close that you can almost touch
them. Resist the urge, however,
because you could damage or
abrade the delicate skin of these
fish, thus permitting harmful
parasites to attach among their
scales. Going down a little farther,
near the saddle between the two
reefs, you'll find a cave opening
into the wall that offers shelter to
another marvel of Shark Reef:
a gigantic grouper almost two
meters long, which usually lies on
the bottom of the cavern's
entrance. If you move slowly,
you'll be able to come close to this
sort of prehistoric monster before
it retreats to the maze of its den.
In December and January,
responding to the irresistible urge
to reproduce, gray sharks gather
here to mate, and can be seen as
they perform their courting rituals.
When you reach the sandy
plateau, you'll see a group of jacks
in compact formation near the
wall, and a dense school of batfish
suspended in the blue depths.
Along the reef, at all depths, you'll
see the usual activity of the whole
range of colorful coral fish,

including red groupers, parrotfish, butterflyfish and spotted angelfish. Due to its special position, almost any encounter is possible at Shark Reef. You'll have magical moments, but never forget the usual safety rules: check your underwater computer regularly, because the clear water and beauty of the sea bed may tempt you to go beyond your depth and time limits.

The best diving depth is between 20 and 25 meters.

A single dive at Shark Reef will not be enough for photographers. You can use any kind of lens, but perhaps a wide-angle may be preferable, as it permits close-up shots of large portions of the reef.

F

E

G

E, G - You may see a unique sight around Shark Reef in the summer, when thousands of red snappers (Lutjanus bohar) gather along the wall in groups so dense that they look like a solid mass.

F - A diver approaches a school of batfish (Platax sp.). As can be seen, a semi-closed circuit breathing system means no air bubbles and no noise, thus making it possible to get so close to the fish that they will accept you as a member of the school.

H - A splendid gray reef shark (Carcharhinus amblyrhynchos) is accompanied in its ceaseless wanderings by a group of rainbow runners (Elagatis bipinnulata).

H

JOLANDA REEF

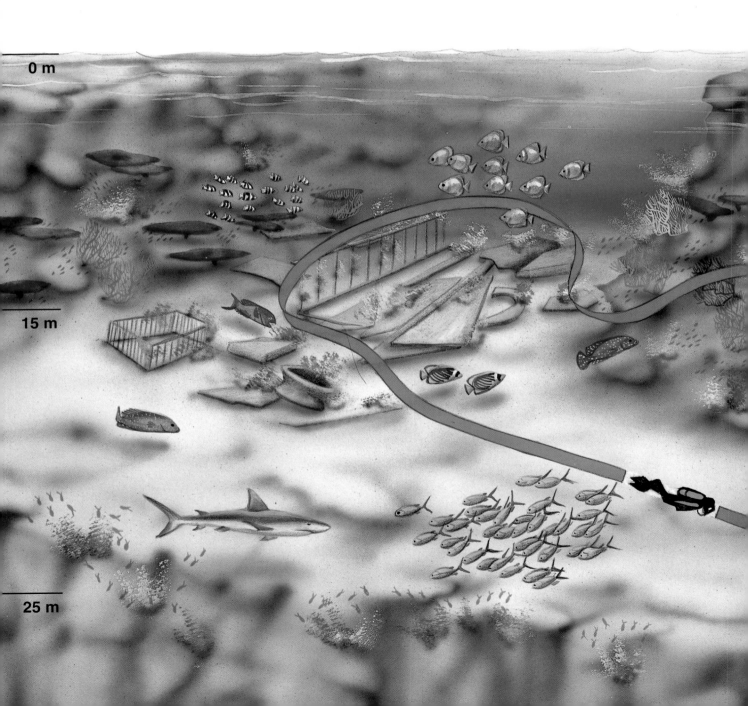

0 m

15 m

25 m

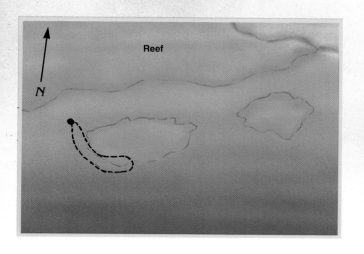

Reef

N

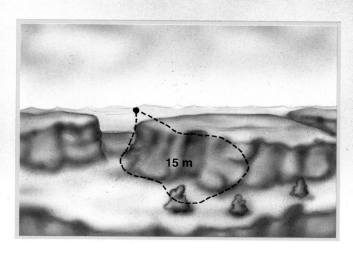

15 m

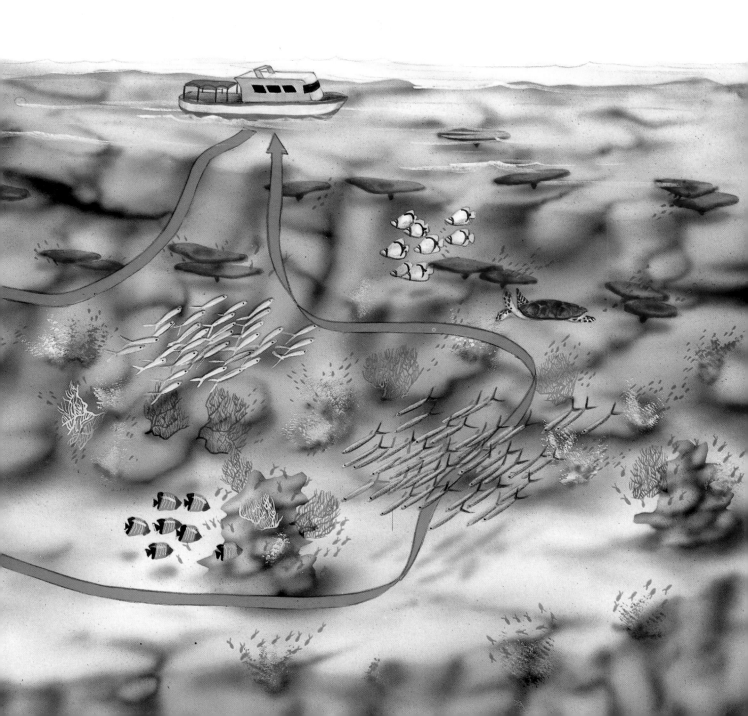

Jolanda is the southernmost of the two coral towers located at the tip of the Sinai Peninsula, where the waters from the Gulf of Aqaba, mixing with those of the Gulf of Suez, create one of the most spectacular biological areas in the world for scuba divers. The reef takes its name from the Cypriot merchant ship that ran aground here in 1981. The ship remained perched on the edge of the abyss until 1987, when it was swallowed by the sea after a violent storm, leaving part of its cargo on the sandy shallow bottom west of the reef. Today, at a depth of about 10-14 meters, you can see

A

B

C

D

A - A group of snappers (Lutjanus sp.) swims near the metallic structures of what was once a container. These fish are easy to approach and make an interesting subject for photographers.

B - Although the wreckage of the ship certainly does not beautify the area, it is interesting to note how it has been taken over by the underwater world in just a few years, forming true biological niches.

C - A brilliant lemon yellow jackfish swims near the sea bottom, probably hunting some small fish. This type of jackfish can change color from yellow to silver.

tangled cables, bundles of long poles and what remains of the two containers that contained toilets, sinks and bathtubs. The remains, of little interest in themselves, are nevertheless adorned with the luxuriant corals that have colonized them and the colorful fish that now live near them. The area is easy to explore even from the surface, making this an entertaining area for snorkelers as well.
The area is a 40 minute sail south of Sharm el-Maya.
You can moor your boat to the permanent mooring lines anchored to the bottom, but the best way to enjoy Jolanda Reef is to circumnavigate the imposing coral tower in a drift dive. Check the direction of the current before you decide which way your dive will proceed.
If you decide to enter the water from your moored boat, tie it to a loop in the line on the western side of the reef, and once you've entered the water, briefly explore the remains of the *Jolanda* and then, keeping the wall to your left, head to the plateau at a

depth of 25 meters and surface near the reef to return to your boat. If you are experienced enough to drift dive, jump into the water near the saddle between Jolanda Reef and Shark Reef. You'll immediately see numerous jackfish with their characteristic silvery color spattered with dark spots, as they patrol this area in search of prey. Head south, with the wall to your right, and on the sea floor you'll see several low coral mushrooms covered with alcyonarians, in the shelter of which are exceptionally large morays. These peaceful beasts will often leave their lairs to sinuously swim among the protuberances on the sea floor. If you look carefully at the sandy and detrital areas with no corals, you can see timid gobies peering out of the holes in the floor in which they live. These small, colorful fish have an extraordinary symbiotic relationship with a tiny shrimp that shares their homes.
The shrimp, which is nearly blind, is warned of possible

predators through movements of the fish's tail, while the crustacean regularly cleans the hole where they both live. Schools of batfish hover in the blue depths; sometimes so many of them gather in compact formation that they look like a silvery wall. These elegant, circular-shaped fish move continuously at various depths, following the flow of the plankton carried in by the current. When you reach a depth of 25 meters, you'll see a large gorgonian with a beautiful, delicately-colored alcyonarian growing on it, and a little farther off a formation of grape corals that looks like an enormous cluster of greenish-gray grapes. If you carefully examine these strange round forms, you'll see tiny, lavender-colored shrimp among them. Go on to a plateau dotted with coral pinnacles carpeted with soft corals, around which swim swarms of red anthias, spotted angelfish and groups of yellow goatfish. Turn toward the open sea and go to the outer edge of the plateau, where the drop-off plunges vertically into a vertiginous blue abyss, and you'll see a moving, silvery mass: an enormous school of large barracudas that often forms a vortex that runs from the sea floor to the water's surface. The sight is breathtaking, even more so because rather than swimming away, the barracudas simply ignore divers and continue to glide around them. Leave the edge of the terrace and head for the remains of the *Jolanda*, examining a meadow of soft corals from which rise imposing formations of umbrella corals. On the sandy floor there are crocodile fish and spotted stingrays, and in the other parts of the cargo ship swim red groupers and numerous parrotfish. Clusters of colorful alcyonarians hang from the metallic frame skeletons of what were once containers, accompanied by slow-swimming, yellow-pink breams. Finish your dive by exploring the reef at a

depth of 4-5 meters, in an area full of crevices and small cracks where you can see turtles and turkeyfish mingled with hundreds of sergeant majors, their white bodies traversed by characteristic vertical black bands. Underwater photographers will find it truly hard to decide which lens to use, because any type is suitable here. I personally recommend using a wide-angle lens which is not too extreme, such as the 20 mm, which is versatile enough to be used for many different kinds of shots. Pay attention to your position and the power of the flash, and remember that fish like jacks and batfish are extremely reflective.

D - Numerous species of fish, including snappers (Lutjanus sp.) and lunartail groupers (Variola louti), have found an ideal habitat among the structures of the wreck of the Jolanda.

E - Sometimes batfish (Platax teira) make vertical formations that seem to rise to reach the surface of the sea.

F - A diver who has clearly mastered position techniques hangs suspended in the blue depths as he watches a school of jackfish (Caranx sp.) reflecting the sunlight.

G - The walls of the reef are adorned with strangely-shaped coral formations like this red whip coral that looks like a dry bush, but is actually pulsing with life.

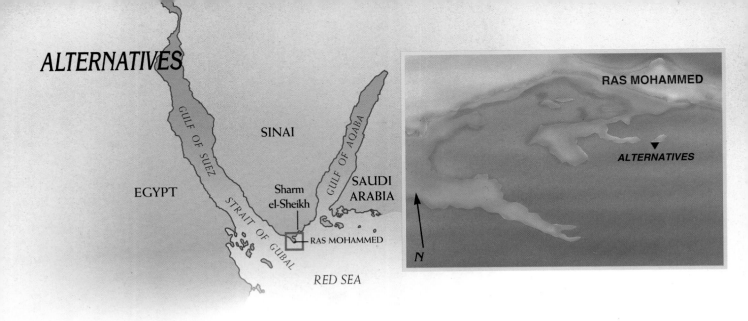

ALTERNATIVES

EGYPT

GULF OF SUEZ

SINAI

GULF OF AQABA

SAUDI ARABIA

Sharm el-Sheikh

STRAIT OF GUBAL

RAS MOHAMMED

RED SEA

RAS MOHAMMED

ALTERNATIVES

N

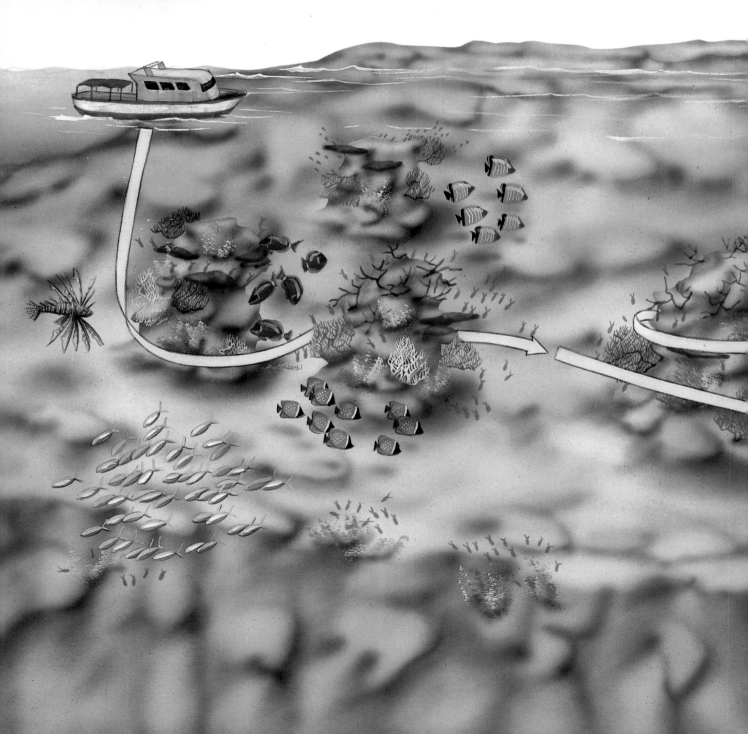

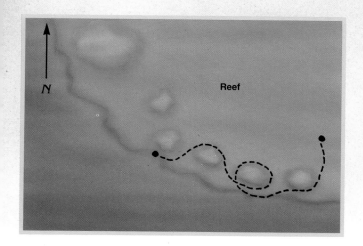

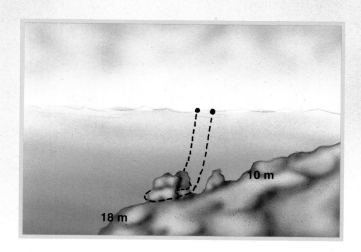

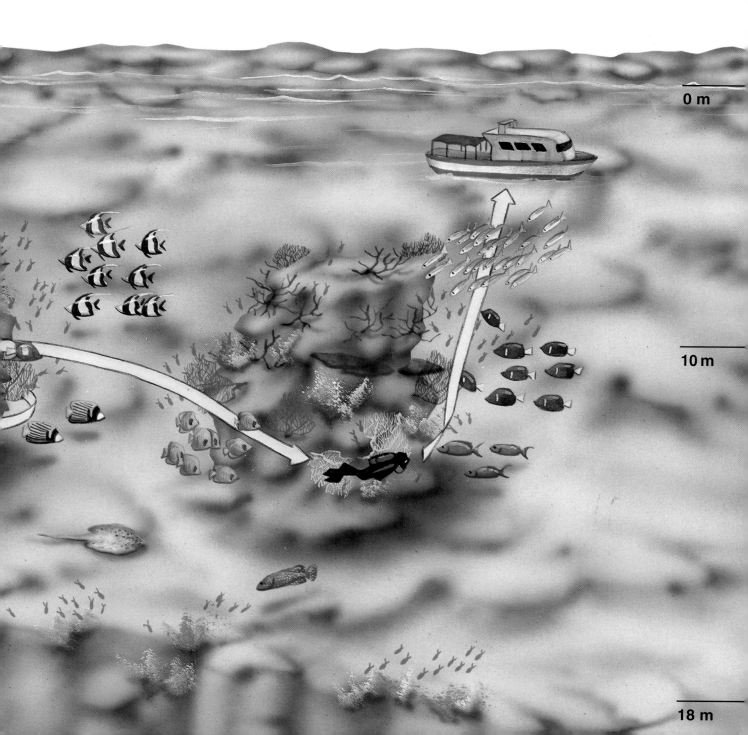

A lternatives, or *saba erg* (seven pinnacles), as it is known by local fishermen, is a series of small emerged coral formations that runs about two miles east to west on the southeast side of Sha'ab Mahmoud. Sha'ab Mahmoud is a long, narrow coral reef which borders a shallow, sandy lagoon west of Ras Mohammed. The western part of the reef is compact, interrupted in only two places: Small Crack and Big Crack passes. To the south, the lagoon is completely open and bordered by the isolated coral towers known to divers as "Alternatives". The area is an hour and a half sail from Sharm el-Maya. When the wind is blowing from the northeast, this area offers

C

A

D

B

A - A crinoid has colonized the outer edge of a gorgonian sea fan and distends its numerous arms in order to capture plankton. Usually these creatures are nocturnal, but in areas swept by currents, they are active during the day as well.

B - Two elegant angelfish (Pomacanthus imperator) swim along the reef which is completely covered by the most incredible and colorful life forms.

C - There are true explosions of light and color around the coral mushrooms; the favorable currents allow hard and soft corals to grow to spectacular sizes.

D - The sandy and detrital areas at the base of the coral towers are an ideal place to look for blue-spotted stingrays (Taeniura lymma).

good shelter and some very entertaining dives, especially for underwater photographers. The coral mushrooms are at the edge of the sandy lagoon, and in the inner area it is no more than 10 meters deep, while the wall descends to about 20 meters near the open sea. When the current is running from the north, diving conditions will be excellent, with clear water and the corals at their best. Otherwise, the detritus from the lagoon makes visibility poor. Given the conformation of the sea bottom, you should use drift dive techniques in order to explore more of the reef. For those who prefer to leave the boat anchored, there is a mooring line. A trip to Alternatives is suitable for divers with any level of experience. Enter the water at the fifth or sixth pinnacle, counting from the east, and proceed by keeping the deepest part to your right. Go around each coral foundation to explore all the walls of these formations. Some are 5-6 meters in diameter, while others are smaller but just as full of life. The towers are not too distant from each other, and when visibility is good, you will see the next formation as soon as you leave the previous one. The coral mushrooms are decorated with blooms of alcyonarians in a thousand colors, and by dark red gorgonians with white out-turned polyps that look like snowflakes. If you look carefully among the polyps of the alcyonarians, you can see tiny little camouflaged crabs. On the upper part there are dense tangles of dark red sponges covered with beautiful yellow and black nudibranchs. Turkeyfish move elegantly at the water's surface, stalking groups of glassfish and vibrating their long, feather-like pectoral fins. Dozens of anthias swim around a formation of fire coral, creating spectacular plays of color. In the crevices are numerous *Tubastrea* corals and curious gobies peeping from their shelters. The entire array of coral fish is here: red groupers, trunkfish, parrotfish, surgeonfish and butterflyfish. Blue-spotted stingrays lie in the sand at the base, and gray morays with their distinctive yellowish-gray bodies and black-spotted heads peer out of their lairs. Pay special attention to the sandy areas with no corals, where you may see the leopard sharks which usually lie on the bottom. Needless to say, these are thrilling sights. This dive, which is excellent for photographers, is good for getting pictures of fish in their own habitat.

The best lenses are certainly those considered standard, such as the 35 or 50 mm. If you have a camera in an underwater case, the best lens is a 28-70 mm zoom, which can be used for seascapes as well as close-ups. Wide-angle lenses can also be used, especially for splendid shots of alcyonarians, gorgonians and sponges.

E

F

G

H

I

E - A turkeyfish (Pterois sp.) *advances toward the photographer, almost as if posing. In the late afternoon these marvelous members of the Scorpaenidae family are easy to spot as they leave the places where they usually lie in wait and dance elegantly in the open water.*

F - Although the *bright colors of the sponges and alcyonarians are captivating, once in a while you should examine the sandy areas, where leopard sharks (Stegostoma fasciatum) often can be seen lying on the sea floor.*

G - The gray moray (Siderea grisea) *is the most common species in the Red Sea. Often more than one individual lives in the same lair, from which they come out only at night.*

H - Many small, *skillfully camouflaged crustaceans live among the polyps of the alcyonarians. Macrophotography fans will find Alternatives a true paradise.*

I - A cleaner fish *intently performs its services on the snout of a squirrelfish (Sargocentron spiniferum).* Little *cleaner fish play an extremely important role in reef life: they remove harmful parasites from the skin of fish who could not free themselves of parasites alone. They live in areas known as "cleaning stations," which are also visited by sea giants like the mantas.*

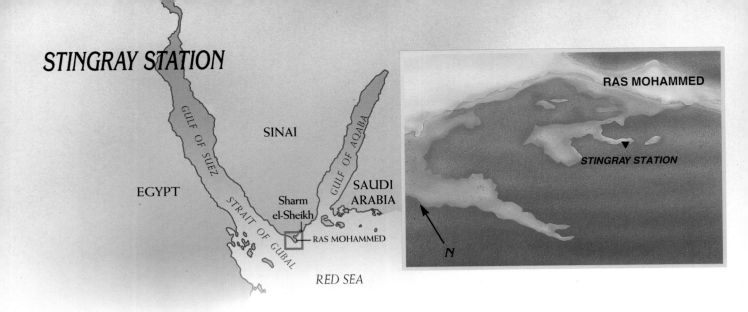

STINGRAY STATION

GULF OF SUEZ

STRAIT OF GUBAL

GULF OF AQABA

SINAI

EGYPT

Sharm el-Sheikh

SAUDI ARABIA

RAS MOHAMMED

RED SEA

RAS MOHAMMED

STINGRAY STATION

N

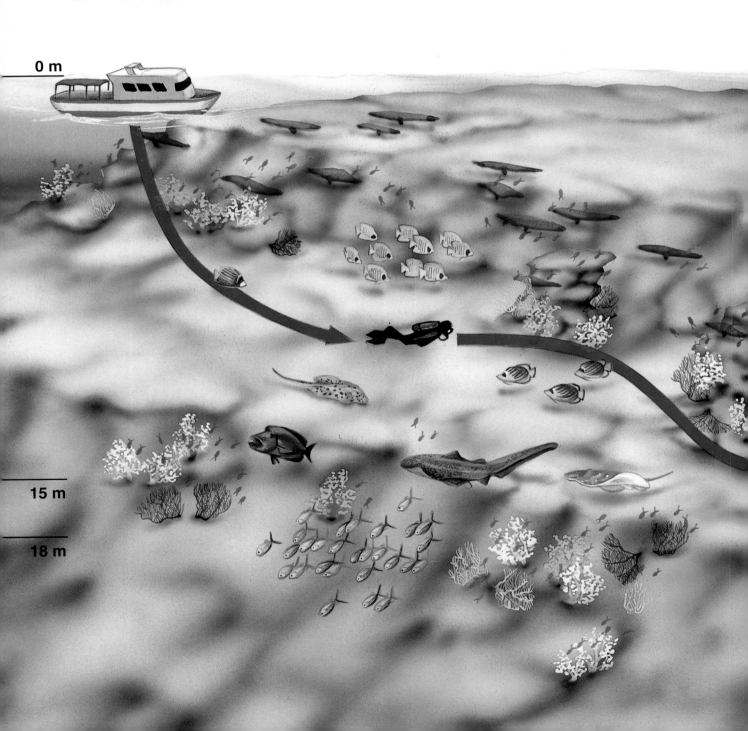

0 m

15 m

18 m

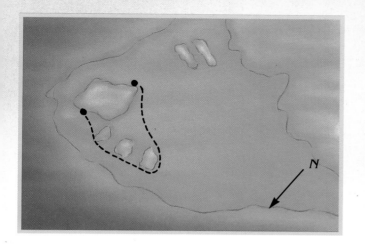

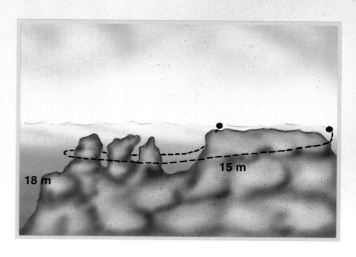

18 m

15 m

N

T he last coral formation west of the labyrinthine coral complex at Alternatives is known as Stingray Station. During the spring, you will see many types of rays in this region, where they gather on the sandy areas of the western branch of Sha'ab Mahmoud, perhaps in order to reproduce. The most common species is certainly the blue-spotted stingray, but large feathertail rays have also been sighted. These members of the *Dasyatidae* family, with disk-shaped bodies that may reach more than 2 meters in width, are easily recognizable by the large lobe at the end of their long, thin tails. These animals feed by following the tides; at high tide

B

A

C

they go to shallower waters to feed on worms, small fish, crabs and other small crustaceans, which they uncover with rapid movements of their mantles. The diving area is about a one hour sail away from the landing stage at Sharm el-Maya; after you reach the Ras Mohammed promontory, turn northwest and skirt the shallow Sha'ab Mahmoud lagoon. You can moor the boat, but it is better to explore Stingray Station in a drift dive. Diving conditions are optimal when the wind is northeasterly with a gentle current from the north, making underwater visibility excellent and the sea calm. The dive usually

D

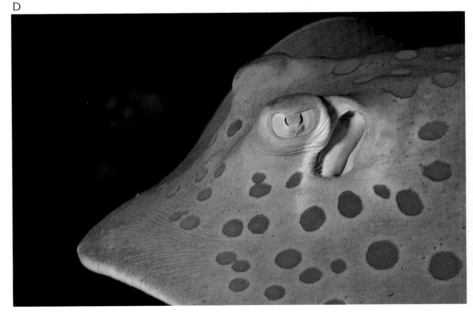

A - Alcyonarians are predator organisms which can capture small crustaceans and other tiny organisms carried in by the current, using their stinging cells and the adhesive mucus that covers the tentacles of their polyps.

B - In the fragile reef ecosystem, each species develops in a way that best exploits the natural resources necessary for its growth.

C - A stingray (Taeniura melanospilos) swims above the sandy floor with elegant wing strokes. It has a fearsome defense weapon: a stinger near the end of its long tail that can be used as a whip to defend itself.

D - The sandy bottom within lagoons or around reefs are full of life, despite the fact that they may seem uninhabited at first sight. The blue-spotted stingray (Taeniura lymma) usually stays buried under the sand.

E - Members of the Scorpaenidae family are true champions of mimicry, and it takes a sharp eye to spot one on the sea floor.

F - Anthias populate every part of the coral reef, from the surface to about 30 meters.

G - As plankton tends to move to shallow depths during the night, after sunset the alcyonarians tend to change their appearance, extending their polyps.

H - Numerous worms looking like a Christmas tree can be seen on this block of coral. The colored part that can be seen protruding from the coral is only the tentacles they use for breathing and eating.

E

F

G

begins from the northwest side of the reef. Keeping the wall to your left, circle around the coral tower until you find yourself in the lagoon. The recommended depth for this dive is between 15 and 18 meters. It is not uncommon to see leopard sharks lazily resting on the sand in the detrital areas with no corals. In addition to stingrays and sharks, you will also see the frenetic life of the coral reef all around you, with continuously moving butterflyfish and surgeonfish, while attached to the walls are gorgonians and dense formations of pale-colored alcyonarians. Pay particular attention to the small clusters of coral, which are often embellished with thick tangles of red sponges;

H

if you look closely, you will see extraordinarily colorful creatures in all shapes and forms which would normally pass unobserved. In the open water, you may see some small humphead wrasses and sparse groups of jacks, constantly on the hunt. Because the landing stages on the coast are relatively distant, scuba diving boats do not often visit this area. Although Stingray Station is an ideal place for close-up photography fans, it also offers spectacular seascape shots. The most colorful subjects are certainly the clumps of red sponges surrounded by swarms of purple anthias. This dive is suitable for all levels of experience.

THE WRECK OF THE DUNRAVEN

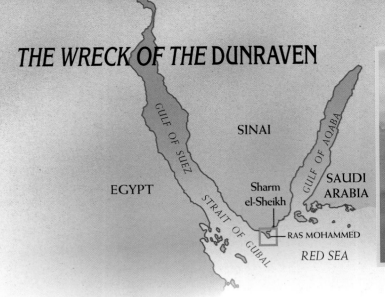

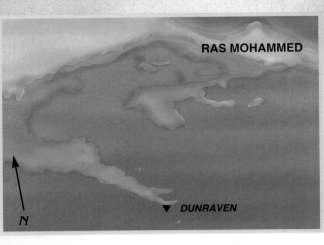

RAS MOHAMMED

N

▼ DUNRAVEN

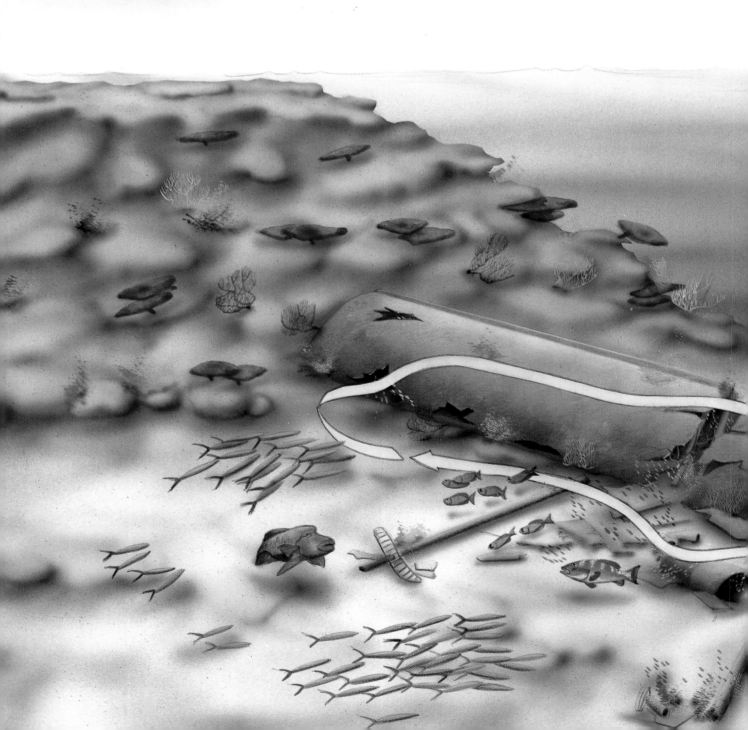

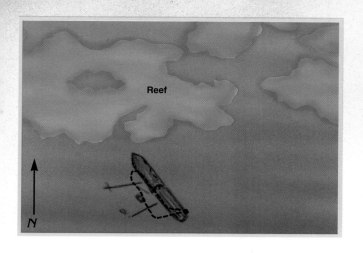

Reef

N

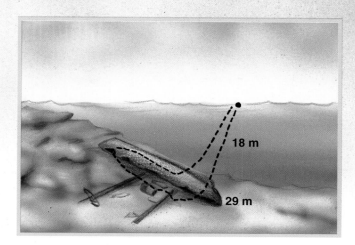

18 m

29 m

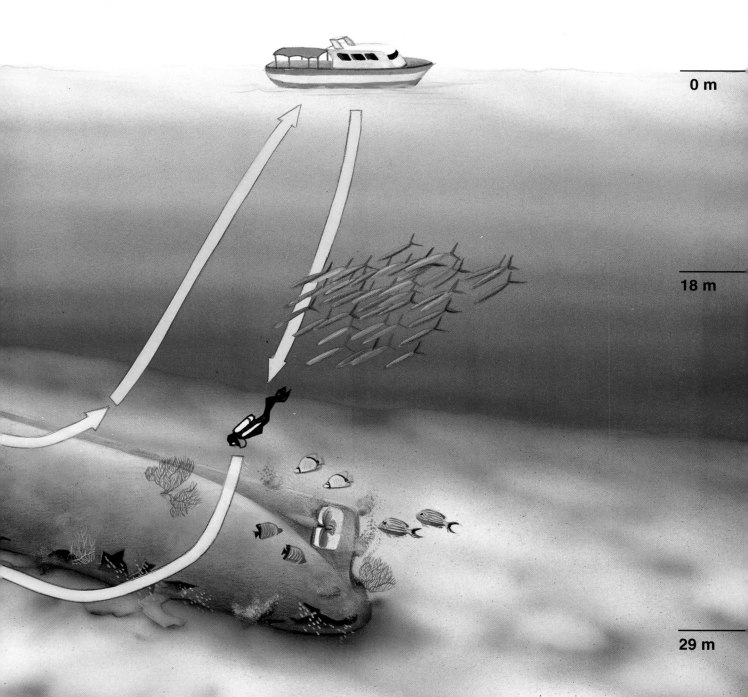

0 m

18 m

29 m

The wreck of the *Dunraven* lies at Beacon Rock, at the southern tip of the group of reefs at Sha'ab Mahmoud. The diving area is about a 2 hour sail from Sharm el-Maya: once you have doubled the cape of Ras Mohammed, head west, and soon you'll see the lighthouse that marks the reef at Beacon Rock. There is a permanent mooring buoy on the outer part of the reef, about 50 meters south of where the ship lies. The constant currents make it inadvisable to dive from the moored boat, unless you have a raft to pick you up. The best solution is to tie the diving boat to the metallic

A

B

C

D

A - A group of butterflyfish (Heniochus intermedius) has staked out its territory among the contorted structures of the wreck, where there are abundant invertebrates to eat.

B - The metallic masses of wrecks provide an excellent support for the growth of corals.

C - Some groupers have mimetic colors that make them almost invisible when they lie in ambush. Others, like this Plectropomus, *have colors that are hard not to notice.*

structure of the wreck, thus avoiding damage to the coral concretions which now cover the entire ship. There are two loops of heavy cord already fixed to sturdy beams that you can use for this purpose.
The *Dunraven*, 82 meters long and about 10 meters wide, was a steamship with a double propulsion system that used both sails and steam. Built in England in 1870, it was used to transport cargo from India to Europe.
In April 1876, on a return voyage from Bombay with a load of wool, cotton and wood, it broadsided the semi-emerged reef from the right and broke into three parts. A fire broke out on board and the cargo burned for hours, until the hull overturned and landed upside-down on the sea bed about 25 meters deep. This area is constantly swept by currents, and visibility is not always good due to the detritus and sediments on the bottom, but the water inside the wreck is always fairly clear. Begin the dive from the stern, and just a few meters down

you'll see the outline of the keel, which is still in perfect condition. The most interesting part is the propeller and the rudder, which are turned upward and are covered with colorful alcyonarians, around which swim parrotfish and butterflyfish. The aft section, which is resting on the sea bed about 30 meters deep, and the left broadside are in perfect condition and thickly colonized by various types of corals. This area is a must for macrophotography fans. There are also numerous small crustaceans and nudibranchs in an endless variety of shapes and colors. It is not particularly difficult to enter the wreck, as the rips in the right broadside are quite large. A fair amount of light filters in from the openings, but for a more thorough exploration you'll need a good underwater flashlight. Enter from the opening near the stern, and you'll see squirrelfish and large groupers swimming among the contorted wreckage. From a dark area

under a bulkhead the head of
a large moray appears,
surrounded by darting cleaner
fish. A large staghorn coral has
grown in the central portion,
where it partially obstructs a hole,
creating beautiful plays of light.
In the tangle of cables and
wreckage which must once
have been the engine room,
you can see a boiler and a large
smokestack, with swarms of
glassfish swimming all around.
Go back out through the rip
in the center, where a school
of black-spotted yellow grunts
hovers, and then re-enter through
the opening at the prow.
Walls of glassfish swim among
the metallic walls, reflecting
the sunlight in golden flashes.
About a dozen turkeyfish circle
in the middle of this shining
swarm, their pectoral fins open
like wings, in a scene that
underwater photographers will
be unable to resist.
Outside the wreck of the
Dunraven, the two masts rest
on the sea floor toward the open
water; you can still see the top
of one of them, covered with
corals. If you look out to the
open sea, you may see
humphead wrasses, barracudas
and, in the winter, mantas.
Return to the reef, moving
above the prow, which is about
18 meters from the surface.
Once you approach the wall,
which ascends gently, you'll see
crocodile fish and a large variety
of coral fish, with large
gorgonians growing on some
of the protuberances of the sea
floor. After you make your usual
safety stop at a depth of 5
meters, surface near the reef
and swim to the boat from the
surface. This dive is especially
good for seascape photos.
Within the wreck in particular,
if you use wide-angle lenses you
can capture highly effective
images by using the shiny wall
of glassfish as a subject.
For macrophotography, if your
subjects are static, you can get
good results with extension tubes
as well. Dives on the wreck of the
Dunraven are suitable for divers
with any level of experience.

E

F

G

*D - Marine
organisms, corals,
sponges and fish
have taken over the
structures of the
wreck, creating
vivid palettes of
color that grow
even brighter when
illuminated by an
underwater
flashlight, which
you should always
carry during this
type of dive.
Here is depicted
an angelfish
(Pomacanthus
imperator).*

*E - Thousands of
tiny glassfish live
protected within
the wreckage,
making the
encrusted walls
of the ship sparkle
with brilliant
silvery and golden
reflections.*

*F - Exploring
a shipwreck
is always exciting,
but be very careful
of the stability
of the structures,
which may be
precarious due
to corrosion.
During the
exploration of the
wreck one can find
a superb coral
grouper
(Cephalopholis
miniata).*

*G - All the
inhabitants of the
coral reef, including
small crustaceans
slithering in the
darker areas, can
be seen in the now
unrecognizable
structures.*

SMALL CRACK

EGYPT
GULF OF SUEZ
SINAI
GULF OF AQABA
SAUDI ARABIA
Sharm el-Sheikh
STRAIT OF GUBAL
RAS MOHAMMED
RED SEA

RAS MOHAMMED
SMALL CRACK
N

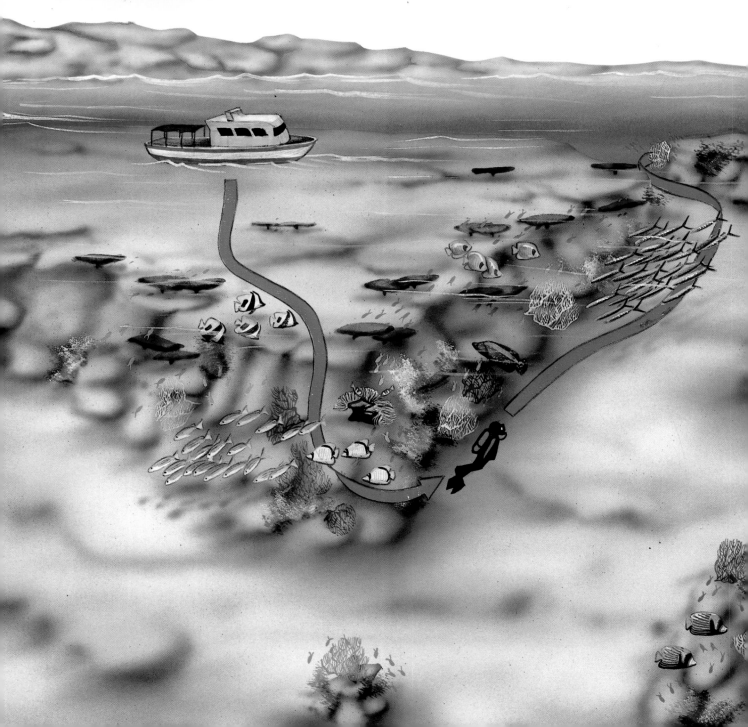

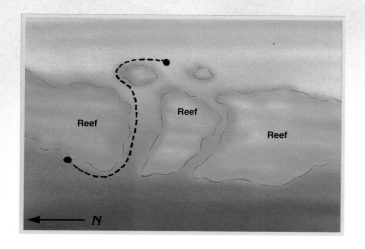

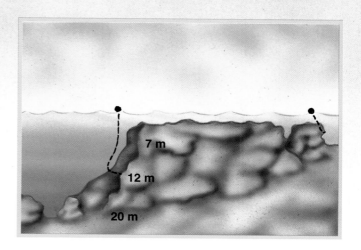

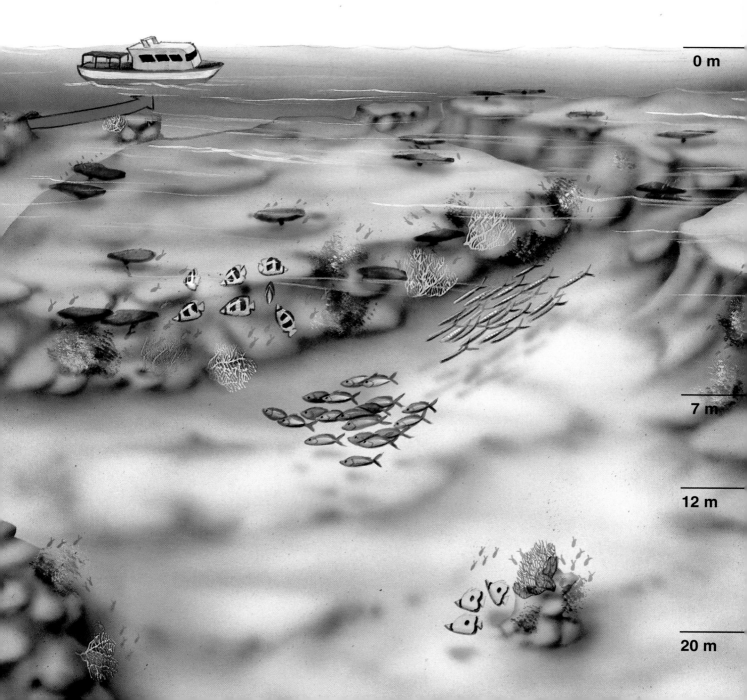

0 m

7 m

12 m

20 m

This diving area is about a two hour sail from Sharm el-Maya. After doubling the cape of Ras Mohammed, head toward the Beacon Rock lighthouse, which marks the southernmost point of the long reef that breaks off from the Sinai coast and is known as Sha'ab Mahmoud. From this point, follow the reef to the northwest until you come to a passageway that leads into the lagoon. This is Small Crack. As there is no place for the boat to moor except in the lagoon, you must use drift dive techniques here. The area is not often frequented by the daily boats that leave from

B

A - Delicate gorgonians with rather unusual colors and forms grow in some of the crevices.

B - Do not be deceived by the apparent slowness of turkeyfish (Pterois sp.). When they attack, they are capable of movements faster than the human eye can perceive.

C - The most interesting area for underwater photographers is certainly the narrow channel that leads from the open sea into the lagoon.

D - The boxfish (Ostracon cubicus) is quite shy and can only be approached at night. It is rather awkward and is one of the strangest inhabitants of the reef.

A

C

Sharm el-Sheikh, while it is popular with a number of cruise boats, which spend the night in the calm waters of the lagoon. During my last dive in this part of the Strait of Gubal, I was accompanied by a friend, who can be considered one of the pioneers of diving around the Sinai coast and it is thanks to his experience and knowledge of these waters that I was able to see some of the true jewels of this reef. The support raft will drop you off in the water about 100 meters north of the small pass. At this point, the wall of the reef descends to a depth of 25 meters, at about a 45° angle from the surface.

D

E - Under optimal conditions, the constructor polyps of the so-called hard corals develop in contorted branching formations that look like stone trees.

F - The clown anemonefish (Amphiprion bicinctus) takes refuge among the stinging tentacles of the anemone, from which it is immune. In exchange for this effective protection, the anemonefish keeps butterflyfish from preying on the anemone.

G - A hawkfish (Paracirrhites forsteri) caught in a classic ambush position. The hawkfish is sedentary and usually lies in wait on the corals. When any fish deceived by its immobility comes too close to its mouth, it will dart forward and grab it.

H - During the spring you can see large groups of humpback red snappers (Lutjanus gibbus), which probably gather for purposes of reproduction.

G

E

H

F

A gentle current will carry you south, and as you reach a depth of 29 meters you will see a school of red snappers, who will let you approach them. Occasions like these will make you fully appreciate the large frames of lenses like the 15 mm *Nikonos* or the 20 mm amphibious camera. A servoflash will help to minimize the shadows created by the main flash, held back in order to increase the breadth of the light. Visibility is excellent, and I feel that the best part of the wall is at about 20 meters deep, where the largest gorgonian sea fans are located. Delicate, pale lilac-colored alcyonarians often grow at the bases of these splendid sea fans. Small groups of parrotfish and innumerable pairs of butterflyfish swim around the protuberances of the wall. My diving partner calls my attention to a distant spot of indistinct yellow; we approach and discover a dense school of blue-striped snappers, who may be gathered in this area to mate: this is a rather rare sight in the Red Sea. We move to a depth of 14 meters, where we survey an enormous gorgonian and a large *Acropora* umbrella beneath which grows a beautiful red alcyonarian. We come to the entry to the small pass and

A

rise to a depth of 7-8 meters, just in time to see an unusual anemone with red tentacles. I immediately pick up the camera, equipped with a 105 mm lens, and take several photographs of the anemonefish hiding within it. When I later look at the slides, I am disappointed to see no trace of the red anemone. We enter the narrow passageway that leads into the lagoon, where the white sand bottom imbues the area with an incredible light.

A - A humphead wrasse (Cheilinus undulatus) swims together with a silver jackfish (Caranx sp.).

B - The coral formations near the surface of the Red Sea are full of species that form large colonies of various types. Here one can see a parrotfish hovering on a fire coral formation (Millepora dichotoma).

B

C

E

D

The left wall, which rises to the surface, is perfectly intact, and the work of the coral polyps is absolutely extraordinary. All types of hard corals grow one beside the other in marvelous disarray. We go on a few meters to find Small Crack's main attraction: coral mushrooms growing from the sandy floor within the channel, completely covered with alcyonarians in a thousand colors and forms. The stretch of soft corals is

C - A dense group of humpback red snappers (Lutjanus gibbus) patrols the coral floor in search of prey

D - Blue-striped snappers (Lutjanus kasmira) are nocturnal, and during the day they form large schools that move slowly around the coral pinnacles. Divers can approach them easily.

E - A turkeyfish looks curiously at a photographer as it rests comfortably on a coral.

F - Conditions on the outside wall of the lagoon are ideal for the growth of large gorgonian sea fans.

G - Gorgonians, alcyonarians and sponges transform these sea beds into a true underwater garden.

interrupted only by the yellow and red spots of the encrusting sponges, and dozens of red coral groupers emerge from the small cracks, a delight for the eyes.
Underwater photographers could stay down here for hours, kneeling on the sand and creating countless new shots. I use my last two photos on a school of small barracudas suspended at the surface. We surface almost under the boat's transom as it lies

H

F

G

I

anchored to a mooring buoy in the lagoon.
Small Crack is a dive for everyone, as long as the current is not too powerful. The dive is best when the current is running south, because the most interesting part of the outer wall is north of the pass. Divers should be especially careful of their position, especially near the coral mushrooms in the pass.

H - The pass at Small Crack contains several isolated formations that look like large blocks of coral. The walls of these blocks have been colonized by vividly colored encrusting sponges.

I - An adult masked butterflyfish. Younger individuals are easily recognizable by the noticeable dark spot on the posterior end.

THE SHAG ROCK WRECK

EGYPT

SINAI

GULF OF SUEZ

GULF OF AQABA

STRAIT OF GUBAL

SAUDI ARABIA

Sharm el-Sheikh

RAS MOHAMMED

RED SEA

SHA'AB ALI

SHAG ROCK

N

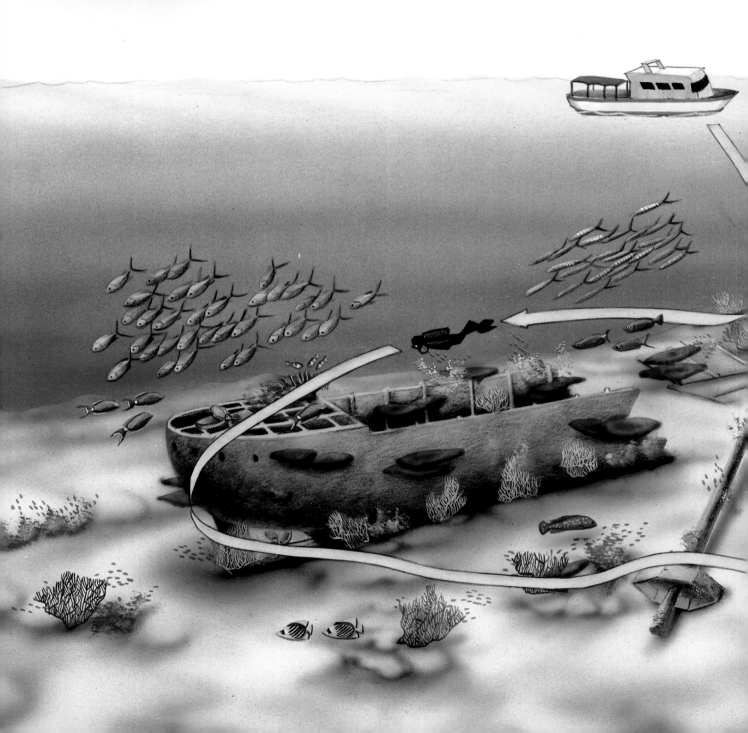

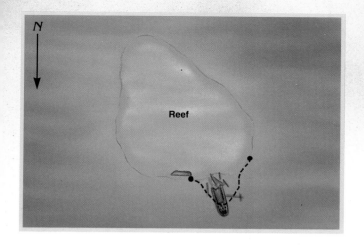

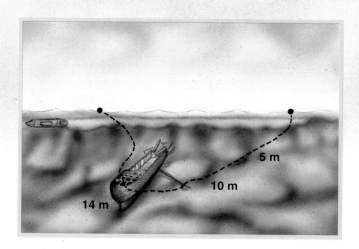

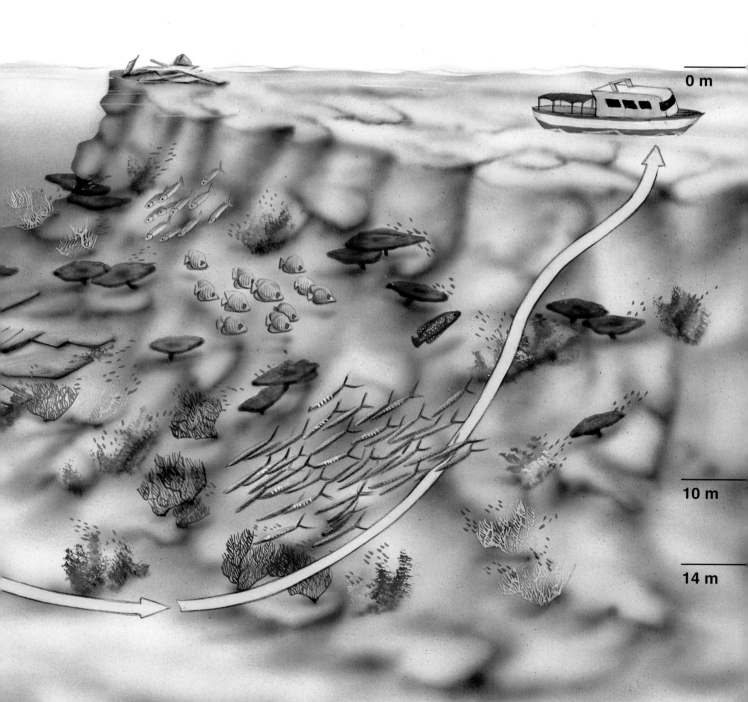

A - Dives on shipwrecks are usually best left to expert divers, but an underwater trip to the Shag Rock wreck can be enjoyed by anyone, due to the relatively shallow depth and the lack of any dangers in the area.

B - Wrecks are often home to many fish, like this moray (Gymnothorax sp.).

This diving area is located to the far south of the Sha'ab Ali coral complex, three hours from Sharm el-Sheikh in the middle of the Strait of Gubal and west of the Sinai Peninsula. Shag Rock is a round coral formation that rises almost to the surface. There is a lighthouse on its far southeast side, and on the north side, scattered on the upper reef, are the few remains of the wreck of a fishing boat. The currents that flow in from

C

A

B

D

the north past Shag Rock are sometimes so powerful that the dive becomes impossible. This area is popular with cruise boats, which have a permanent mooring area on the southern part of the reef. The dive's major attraction is the wreck of the *Sarah H.*, a cargo ship that collided with the reef and sank in upright position at a depth of 15 meters, on a sea bed that slopes down gently in the northern part of Shag Rock.

C - A cloud of golden glassfish reflect warm flashes of light within the Sarah H. *near a rip in the starboard broadside.*

D - Gorgonian sea fans have attached to the sides of what were once the holds of the ship.

E - Numerous species live protected in the thousand crevices formed by the sunken ship, like this solitary spotted angelfish (Pomacanthus maculosus).

F - The inner walls of the ship are thickly colonized by formations of arborescent alcyonarians, corals which prefer sheltered, dimly lit areas.

I recommend starting the dive from the wreck, after you have checked the strength of the current. The central structures are completely covered with luxuriant formations of hard corals, including numerous *Acropora* umbrellas.
In a rift in the central part swim crowds of glassfish, closely watched by redmouth groupers. On the upper deck, you can see a large reserve propeller, now nearly hidden by coral concretions. Inside what was

G

E

F

H

once the hold there are beautiful gorgonians that offer lovely camera shots, perhaps with a diver in the background. The quarter-deck hosts a pair of anemones with their ever-present clown anemonefish, and its structures are covered with a carpet of brown algae. This is the most photogenic and interesting area of the wreck. Many red groupers who have chosen this wreck as their home swim up to divers confidently, and almost seem to pose for

G - An alcyonarian has colonized the metallic structures of the wreck of the Sarah H.

H - A red coral grouper (Cephalopholis miniata), perhaps intrigued by the unusual movements of the photographer, comes out of its safe refuge within the wreck.

A

photographs. Numerous sohal surgeonfish come and go incessantly among the frames, now corroded by time. Photographers will find this section quite interesting due to the lovely plays of light and shadow and because it is so easy to approach the fish. Don't forget to look among the algae to discover nudibranchs or beautiful gobies peeping out. The wreck's stern is resting on a sea bed 14 meters deep. On its right side a large gorgonian has grown near the propeller, and often a big grouper can be seen here. When you have finished exploring the wreck, continue your dive on the west

B

D

C

A - Surgeonfish (Acanthurus sohal) *continuously move through the aft structures, ceaselessly coming and going from the holds. These strong swimmers can keep their position in their own territory even when currents are strong and will defend it aggressively from other surgeonfish.*

B - *Usually it is not difficult to photograph fish within a wreck: perhaps feeling more protected by the boat, they are less suspicious of divers and are easier to approach. Here is a spotted angelfish* (Pomacanthus maculosus).

C - *Two cleaner fish take care of a surgeonfish as they move rapidly along its skin removing parasites.*

side of Shag Rock, keeping the wall to your left and moving along the reef that descends almost vertically to a depth of about 25 meters. As this area is regularly swept by currents, you may encounter pelagic fish such as sharks, jackfish and barracudas, so don't forget to keep an eye on the open sea. The reef offers beautiful gorgonians and areas covered with thick alcyonarians. Encounters with small groups of wrasses are common, as they usually stay out of the current by taking shelter behind various protrusions on the sea floor. The area is frequented by

E

numerous turtles, which are actually not very sociable and thus difficult to photograph. Wide-angle lenses are best for photographing underwater wrecks, and will give the picture greater depth. Those who prefer macrophotography will find numerous subjects within the hold, from small gobies to brightly colored shrimp.
You should dive onto the *Sarah H.* early in the day, as the current usually begins to increase around noon. When the current is weak, this dive is suitable for divers with any level of experience.

F

G

D - The vivid coral fish, the garish colors of the alcyonarians and the other coral forms have softened the drama inherent in shipwrecks.

E, G - Currents may be quite powerful along the north side of the wall, creating ideal conditions for pelagic fish, who, their snouts to the current, await their prey. Barracudas and jackfish are always spectacular and thrilling sights, especially when they form such tight groups that they seem like silvery walls.

F - You can explore the wall at Shag Rock after you examine the shipwreck. It contains pleasant coral seascapes and is full of animal life. Here is a small group of black-spotted grunts (Plectorhynchus gaterinus).

135

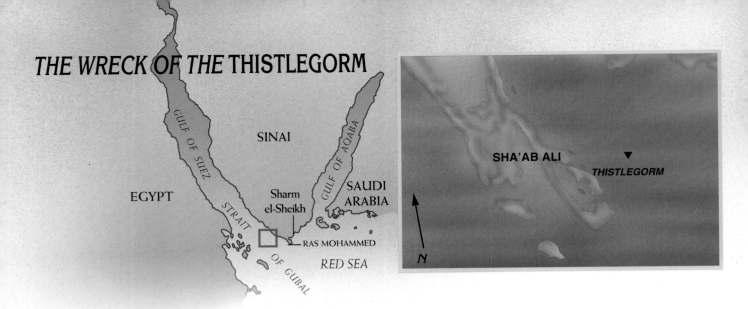

THE WRECK OF THE THISTLEGORM

GULF OF SUEZ

SINAI

GULF OF AQABA

EGYPT

STRAIT

Sharm el-Sheikh

SAUDI ARABIA

RAS MOHAMMED

OF GUBAL

RED SEA

SHA'AB ALI

▽ *THISTLEGORM*

N

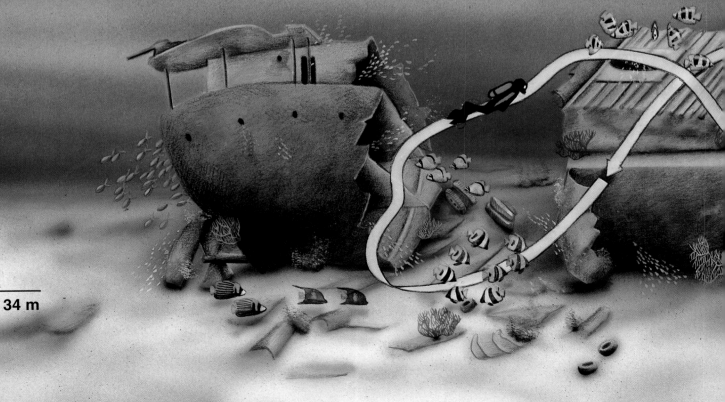

0 m

14 m

34 m

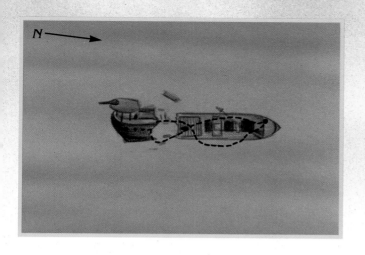

14 m

34 m

N

A

A - The wreck lies 34 meters deep, resting on its left broadside. In this photo a diver is swimming along the stern, giving an idea of the size of the ship.

B - The Thistlegorm's aft section is inclined in a way that leaves the propeller totally exposed.

C - Because of the dimension of the Thistlegorm, we suggest you observe the wreck from a distance before starting the exploration of its structures.

D - During wreck explorations it is always important to have good illumination, in order to better admire the extraordinary life forms that colonize the metal structures.

E - Anthias are a constant presence in shipwrecks, and here they are exceptionally dense near the bow, around the capstans that weighed the anchor chains.

B

C

D

The wreck of the *Thistlegorm* (a Gaelic word that means "blue thistle") is located southeast of Sha'ab Ali, a group of coral formations broken by shallow lagoons 10 miles long and 3 miles wide, located near the mouth of the Gulf of Suez. The area is about a three hour sail from the port of Sharm el-Maya. The ship, which sank in an upright position, lies with its keel on a detrital floor about 34 meters deep, with the prow pointing northwest. Its superstructures are about 14 meters from the surface. The area is swept by sometimes powerful currents that tend to make visibility less than optimal. The wreck was first discovered

E

by Captain Jacques Cousteau 15 years after it sank, during a 1956 expedition of the *Calypso* to the Red Sea. Since then, thousands of scuba divers have explored the *Thistlegorm*, making this cargo ship one of the most popular and well-known sites in the Red Sea. The *Thistlegorm* was launched in England in 1940, and during the war was used primarily to transport provisions from the Americas. For this purpose, it was armed with a cannon and two machine guns, one heavy and the other an anti-aircraft gun on a turret. When it sank, the cargo ship, which was 130 meters long and 18 wide, was on its fourth mission, transporting war materiel for the British army in North Africa. The hold and the two decks contained jeeps, trucks loaded with *BSA* and *Norton* motorcycles, two tanks, two locomotives with cars, torpedoes, rifles and other weapons. In order to make its mission less risky, the British General Staff decided to have it travel to the Suez by circumnavigating Africa, but when it reached Sha'ab Ali it found other ships waiting for the Canal to be cleared, and it had to drop anchor. On the night of October 6, 1941, a German long-range bomber stationed in Crete sighted it and dropped two bombs on it, penetrating the hold and causing a chain of explosions that ripped through the stern, sinking the ship with its 9000 tons of cargo. Today the *Thistlegorm* is completely covered with corals, and thousands of fish of every type have chosen this artificial reef as their home. Its cargo is still clearly visible, and a dive onto this wreck is a fascinating experience that no scuba diver should miss. Because of the size of the wreck, at least two dives will be necessary to explore the ship. Usually the divemaster goes into the water to tie the boat to the metallic structures and check the force and direction of the current. A reference line for the descent and ascent is indispensable for the safety of this excursion, as the currents may change direction and intensity within just a few minutes, and the waves could carry divers far from the boat. The first dive explores the outer part of the wreck: starting at the prow, you will immediately notice the large capstan with its chains, used to weigh the heavy anchors; it is now covered with red alcyonarians surrounded by clouds of anthias. Nearby, a smokestack has been colonized by a carpet of brilliant red encrusting algae, a sight which underwater photographers should not miss. Going toward the stern, on the upper deck, there are two cistern cars with compact groups of batfish swimming nearby. Then comes the mainmast, which has broken in two and lies on the deck, with a minesweeping torpedo lying

F - During the first dive, you should explore the outside structure of the wreck to get an idea of its conformation. The second dive can be used to enter the holds.

G - The atmosphere of a shipwreck is always quite unusual: in any event, you should always follow the directions of your underwater guide, both to explore it to best advantage and to avoid any unnecessary risks.

H - The ladder that led to the forecastle, like the rest of the wreck, is now completely covered with corals that have given new life to this ship that sank so tragically.

I - A dense school of butterflyfish (Heniochus intermedius) hovers near the ripped section of the hull. Completely unafraid of divers, they are easy to approach.

H

F

G

I

on either side. Schools of jackfish and breams, their snouts against the current as they await passing fusiliers, hover near the water's surface in this area. Two train cars can be seen at the sides of the entry to the second hold; they are covered with soft and hard coral concretions. Of particular interest is a formation of colonial anemones which, attached to one of the buffers, will certainly attract macrophotography fans. The bridge, almost completely uncovered, provides an endless source of subjects for close-up photos. Gobies in various forms and colors peep out of the most unlikely openings, brightly colored nudibranchs move slowly on

A - The colorful alcyonarians and red sponges are the most spectacular sights on the wrecks of the Red Sea. This photograph of a smokestack on the forecastle highlights the brilliant colors of the corals which have taken over the structure.

colorful sponges and encrusting yellow *Tubastrea* corals show up beautifully on the rusty wreckage. After passing a contorted metal roof, where you will usually see a crocodile fish, you will come to where the bombs exploded into hold number 4, splitting the hull in two. This is one of the most interesting and photogenic parts of the *Thistlegorm*. Scattered wreckage lies on the sea bed, with two tanks standing out, above which circles a dense group of butterflyfish with long dorsal fins

D

A

B

E

C

and yellow-white and black stripes. Twenty meters from the port side, lying on the bottom, is one of the two locomotives which were loaded on the deck. The aft section is perhaps the most colorful of the whole wreck. Enormous alcyonarians hang from the framework, within which swim silvery, flashing clouds of glassfish and slow-moving angelfish who curiously approach divers, while all around dart fish in every shape and color. Large anemones, colonized by numerous clown anemonefish, grow on the framework. This area is the reign of groupers, with extremely large Malabar groupers and, when the current is weak, giant groupers more than two meters long that weigh 250-300 kilos.
Your second dive will take you into the hold, where you will need a good underwater flashlight. Starting from the bow, enter the first hold, where on the lower level you will find large tires, rubber boots and cases of rifles. On the upper floor there are several

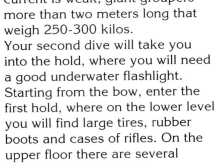

B - Clouds of glassfish, which sometimes overflow to the outside of the holds, always create a pleasant explosion of light. When, illuminated by an underwater flashlight, they sparkle with golden flashes.

C - Two red coral groupers (Cephalopholis miniata) have chosen the cracks created by the contorted wreckage of the sunken ship as their home. Naturally quite curious, they will often approach divers.

D, E - If you can make more than one dive to the wreck, you should reserve at least one for macrophotography. The subjects are practically endless (here are a crustacean and a blenny), and if you look carefully you will find excellent shots among the corals that have encrusted the metallic structures.

automobiles and *BSA* motorcycles. On the lower level of the second hold there are more motorcycles loaded onto trucks, and in the upper portion you will see large number of motorcycles in upright position, as well as some automobiles. This area is extremely fascinating because the vehicles are so well preserved. Both levels of hold number 3 are loaded with bullets and explosives of various sizes and calibers, as well as cases of other materiel. Apart from a few groupers and some swarms of glassfish, the holds are not frequented by many fish. The enormous schools of fish that crowd the waters around the wreck and the colorful, coral formations that encrust the metal structures, along with the variety of cargo that the *Thistlegorm* was transporting, make this dive a must for any scuba diver. Photographers will find so many subjects in so many forms and colors that they will finish their film in no time. Any type of lens is appropriate here.

H

I

F

G

F - Continued ransacking by thoughtless divers has unfortunately impoverished the cargo of the Thistlegorm, *which nevertheless remains one of the most interesting shipwrecks you can visit. Try to resist the temptation to take home a souvenir of your dive: give those who follow you the chance to enjoy the same beautiful things that certainly fascinated you!*

G - The upper deck of hold number one still contains its cargo of Morris *automobiles, their tires with the distinctive sand treads still intact. Even the windshields of some of them are still in one piece.*

H, I - Dozens of BSA *motorcycles are visible in various holds, one next to the other on the flatbed trucks that were to have taken them to the front. In a fast-moving war like that in the desert, motorcycles were useful to connect the front with the area behind the lines.*

SHARM EL-SHEIKH AND ITS SEA LIFE

Due to the elongated, relatively narrow shape and great depth (2850 meters) of the Red Sea, the fascinating coral reefs that characterize it grow more or less parallel to the coast, at the edges of the deep abysses to which they plunge in steep walls, with sea beds less than 50 meters deep occupying only one fifth of the surface. These areas, which receive enough light for vegetation to grow, especially the microalgae *(Zooxanthellae)* that lives in symbiosis with the corals, are always oases teeming with life. Competition for space, which is always greatest on the hard substrata, has led to an extraordinary development of fauna, creating an indescribable "aquarium effect." In just a few square meters you can see a remarkable variety of invertebrates (corals, gorgonians and alcyonarians) and perhaps twenty species of fish, all at the same time.

This description of the Red Sea is an accurate reflection of what can be seen at Sharm el-Sheikh, the gate to the tropics for thousands of scuba divers who often experience both tropical seas and scuba diving for the first time in these waters. Surrounded by reddish deserts that rise toward the mountains of the Sinai Peninsula of Biblical fame, this capital of international scuba diving, located at the border of the true Red Sea and the long Gulf of Aqaba, offers views to first-time visitors arriving by air that are just a taste of the extraordinary dives to come. The coral shallows and the islands in the Strait of Tiran appear in the limpid waters, revealing the edges where the reefs change abruptly and plunge into the blue depths.

The reefs of the Red Sea, which are ever-changing and in continuous growth, even if only by a few millimeters a year, broken and interrupted by fissures and crevices, interspersed with columnar, mushroom and umbrella-shaped formations that edge the sands and underwater meadows, provide an endless number of habitats for marine organisms. Here, some find an ideal refuge as they flee predators, while others lie in wait, hide eggs and their young, or enter into strange symbiotic relationships, like the clown anemonefish and the sea anemone. Every one of them finds food here: herbivores, detrital feeders, omnivores or specialized carnivores. But the coral reef is not just diverse in the forms and sights it offers scuba divers. There are also differences in depth that affect hydrodynamics, illumination or temperature, to give just a few examples. The most common corals divers will see during their excursions are hard corals or *Scleractinia*. Specialists have found over 170 different species of corals in the Red Sea, which makes it understandable why it is impossible to describe them in just a few pages. The most common genera are *Acropora* and *Montipora*, along with *Fungia*, *Porites*, *Favia*, *Favites*, *Stylophora*, *Pavona*, *Leptoseris* and *Cycloseris*.

The distribution of the various species depends primarily on environmental conditions (light, waves and currents), which, after repeated dives, will allow you to recognize the best areas for one or another type of stony coral formation and certain combinations of species. Thus, near the shore you will first find stumpy, branched, light brown colonies of *Stylophora*

(*Pocipolloridae* family), with branches that end in red or purple with white tips. Heading out toward the open sea, there will be large colonies of honeycomb corals, recognizable by the orderly corallites that do indeed look like a honeycomb. The outer, more exposed areas of the reef are dominated by *Acropora* (there are 15 species in the Red Sea), which can be considered the quintessential stony coral. They generally form branched, "staghorn" colonies, which are frequent along the first 10 meters of the reef, facing the open sea. At greater depths *Acropora* tends to broaden, forming plate-shaped, platform-like colonies or umbrella formations, with large flat surfaces supported by a columnar base. Gorgonians and soft corals complete the underwater panorama of Sharm el-Sheikh, as you will quickly discover under the guidance of the divemasters, who will tell you about the gorgonian forests of Ram um Sid and the members of the *Alcyonacea* family, the scientific name for soft corals, which await divers at Thomas Reef. The typical fan-shaped form of gorgonians is too well-known to require description. It may be helpful to note that they grow perpendicular to the current on hard substrata, preferably on the most exposed part of the reef. Some types, known as whip gorgonians, do not have the usual arborescent, branched form, but resemble long steles that curl at the ends. They are not particularly common in the Red Sea, but soft corals certainly are, especially in the more shadowy areas, where cascades of translucent bushes can be seen which are either soft or rubbery to the touch. This is because the calcareous part is limited to the thin spicules incorporated in the main support tissue. These spicules are clearly visible in species in the genus *Dendronephthya*, one of the most common and beautiful of the Red Sea, especially in its arborescent form. These alcyonacea are brightly colored (fuchsia, pink or orange), with polyps clustered

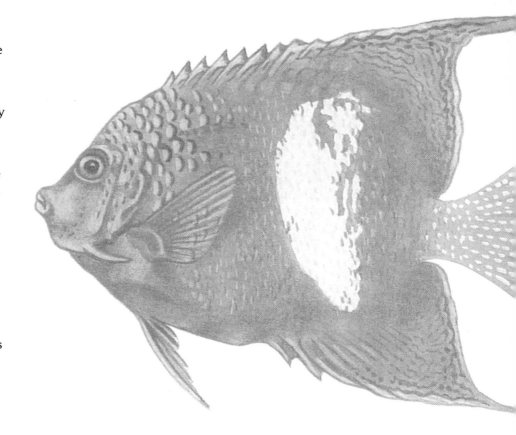

together like flowers, on branches that grow either on a single level or in various directions. These are carnivorous organisms, and thus they most commonly expand at night, when they double or even triple in size, like *Dendronephthya klunzingeri*, which can exceed one meter in height. Surrounded by all these marvels, it may be easy to forget the most basic rules for diving on these sea beds, which for good reason are highly protected at Ras Mohammed, Egypt's largest marine park. Fire corals are perhaps the most dangerous perils, at least until you learn to recognize them. The same can be said for the turkeyfish *(Pterois sp.)*, with their pointed, poisonous fins similar to feathers, and the stonefish, which are just as invisible as they are dangerous. Certainly much less dangerous are the sharks, which in the opinion of many long-time visitors to these waters now seem to have made way for the legions of scuba divers that plunge into these waters every day. In any case, you need only respect the environment and the rules of

recreational diving, swim at a safe distance from the sea floor and never touch anything, and you'll avoid all problems and transform every dive into an exciting experience in the middle of a endless eruption of biodiversity, where the richness of species, forms and colors mingles in incredible, unforgettable ways that you can return to on your next thrilling trip to Sharm el-Sheikh.

GINGLYMOSTOMATIDAE FAMILY ▲

Tawny nurse shark
Nebrius ferrugineus

Tapered body, flattened across the belly. The mouth is set
forward with respect to the eyes. The snout is marked by two
moderately long barbels. The first dorsal fin is larger and taller
than the second ones and the anal fin. The coloring is gray-
brown, and varies in shade from specimen to specimen
according to habitat. This shark is active by night, and
by day it tends to remain in the nooks and crannies
of the coral reef. It feeds on fish and cephalopods.
It measures two to two and a half meters in length.

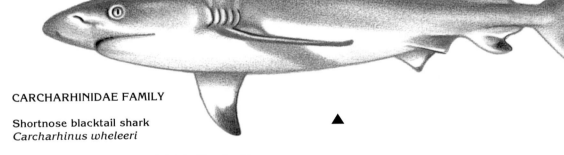

CARCHARHINIDAE FAMILY

Shortnose blacktail shark
Carcharhinus wheleeri

▲

Very similar to the gray reef shark *(Carcharhinus
amblyrhynchos)*, from which it differs by the slightly diverse
coloring. The dorsal fin is slightly sickle-shaped and has a
whitish, somewhat rounded tip, while the back of the tail fin has
a black edge preceded by a bright white stripe. The snout is of
moderate length and is distinctly rounded. The eyes are round.
It measures one and a half to two meters in length. It is not
uncommon at depths between ten and fifty meters.

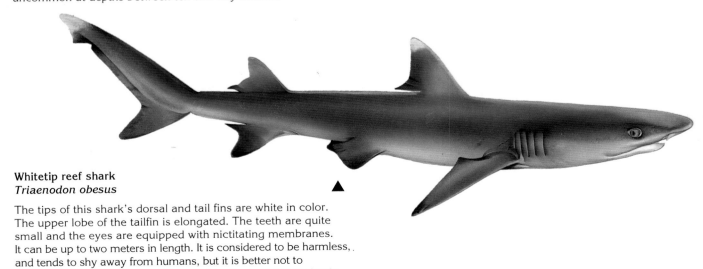

Whitetip reef shark
Triaenodon obesus

▲

The tips of this shark's dorsal and tail fins are white in color.
The upper lobe of the tailfin is elongated. The teeth are quite
small and the eyes are equipped with nictitating membranes.
It can be up to two meters in length. It is considered to be harmless,
and tends to shy away from humans, but it is better not to
underestimate this shark and to consider it - as many maintain -
to be dangerous to humans. It seems to have territorial behavior.

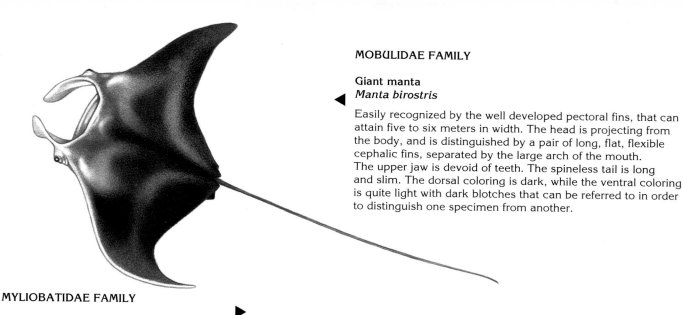

MOBULIDAE FAMILY

Giant manta
Manta birostris

◀

Easily recognized by the well developed pectoral fins, that can attain five to six meters in width. The head is projecting from the body, and is distinguished by a pair of long, flat, flexible cephalic fins, separated by the large arch of the mouth. The upper jaw is devoid of teeth. The spineless tail is long and slim. The dorsal coloring is dark, while the ventral coloring is quite light with dark blotches that can be referred to in order to distinguish one specimen from another.

MYLIOBATIDAE FAMILY

▶

Spotted eagle ray
Aetobatus narinari

This ray can be recognized easily by the pointed and convex head with large eyes and broad lateral spiracles. The body is diamond-shaped and has broad, pointed pectoral fins. The tail, with one, two, or three denticulated spines, is about three times the length of the body. The ventral fins are broad and fleshy. The back is dark in coloring, with many small white spots. The disk-shaped body measures up to two meters in width. It attains a total length of up to two and a half meters. It can also be found in shallow lagoons (one to five meters in depth) on sandy bottoms.

DASYATIDAE FAMILY

Bluespotted lagoon ray
Taeniura lymma

◀

A more or less elongated disk-shaped body, unadorned in the young rays and marked by a series of denticles at the center of the back in the adults. The coloring is grayish brown or yellowish brown on the back, with bluish spots; the belly is light in color. The tail, with one or two poisonous spines at the tip, has bluish stripes along its sides. The disk-shaped body may grow to about one meter in width. At times, the overall length may be greater than two meters. It lives on sandy bottoms at the base of reefs.

SYNODONTIDAE FAMILY
Lizardfish
Synodus variegatus

▼

Elongated body, compressed lengthwise. The head is convex toward the rear base. Eyes in an anterior-dorsal position. The snout is pointed, but short. The mouth is wide, and slightly oblique. The jaws are well developed and equipped with numerous needle-shaped teeth. The coloring is variable, but is generally brownish on the back with more or less distinct red spots on the sides. This fish prefers sandy bottoms where it waits in ambush, poised on its sizable ventral fins.

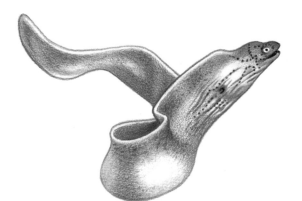

MURAENIDAE FAMILY

Gray moray
Siderea grisea

◀ Small moray with a tapered body and pointed snout, with hard-to-see nares. The mouth is equipped with conical teeth that are more numerous on the upper jaw. The head is brownish, with evident stripes on the back and between the eyes, made up of a series of aligned black points. The rest of the body has a pale brown coloring with violet nuances and brownish marbling. The young are lighter in color. It is not uncommon to see these morays swim in the open on underwater meadowlands. They measure forty to forty-five centimeters in length.

Giant moray
Gymnothorax javanicus

This is the largest of the morays and is fairly common all across the Maldives. The body is powerful, rather tall on the trunk, and ends in a very well developed head. The snout is short. The mouth is wide. The openings of the opercules are large and black and quite evident. The body is marked by three rows of dark brown spots. The tail is reticulated. It can grow to ▶ be as long as two and a half meters.

PLOTOSIDAE FAMILY

Striped eel catfish
Plotosus lineatus

◀ This is a social fish found along coastal reefs and near underwater meadowlands. It is easily recognized by the four barbels that surround its mouth. The second dorsal, the caudal, and the anal fin are connected one to the other. The adults are dark on their backs and have two white longitudinal stripes. The young have bright yellow barbels and fins. The dorsal and pectoral fins have serrated spinous rays connected with poison glands, therefore it is not advisable to handle these fish. They measure from thirty to thirty-five centimeters in length.

FISTULARIIDAE FAMILY

Cornetfish
Fistularia commersonii

A cylindrical body that ends in a long and tubular snout. The dorsal and anal fins are symmetrical and set quite far back. The two central rays of the caudal fin are very fine and elongated. The coloring is variable, due to the remarkable capacity for camouflage which this fish possesses and uses to capture - from ambush - the small prey on which it feeds. It is common to see this fish swim along, hidden by the body of a larger, but harmless, fish, so as to steal up unnoticed upon its prey. This fish measures up to a meter and a half in length.

▼

ANTENNARIIDAE FAMILY

Frogfish
Antennarius coccineus

◀ A stout and rounded body, rather tall, so that this fish is a fairly clumsy swimmer. The fish of this species move slowly and at times make use of their pectoral and ventral fins to "walk" on the seabed. Particularly distinctive is the transformation of the first ray on the dorsal fin, which is used as bait to attract prey. Coloring is quite variable, but always well camouflaged. It lives among coral reefs, at times using its pectoral fins to clutch the coral branches.

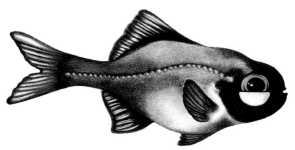

ANOMALOPIDAE FAMILY

Flashlight fish
Photoblepharon palpebratus

Body with an oval shape, a short snout, a truncated forward profile. The eyes are extremely well developed, and beneath them is a large elliptical light-generating organ, which contains luminescent bacteria. This fish is capable of lighting up or extinguishing this organ by raising or lowering a flap of skin. Dark gray in color, this is a typically nocturnal fish. It measures nine to ten centimeters in length.

HOLOCENTRIDAE FAMILY

Blotcheye soldierfish
Myripristis murdjan

Oval body, moderately compressed and high, covered with stinging scales. The first dorsal fin has some ten well developed spinous rays. The eyes are large. The mouth is wide. The coloring is bright red. This is essentially a nocturnal fish, which remains at the entrance to its grotto during the day, as if it were keeping watch. It attains a length of up to thirty centimeters.

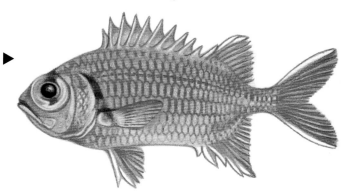

Crown squirrelfish
Sargocentron diadema

Oval body, longer and less tall than that of the *Sargocentron spiniferum* species. The eyes are quite large, as this too is a species with nocturnal habits. The coloring is red, with evident white stripes on the sides. A white band runs around the lower portion of the face as far as to the opercules. The forward section of the dorsal fin is black. It measures twenty-five centimeters in length.

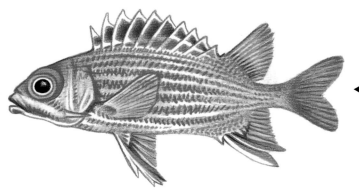

Sabre squirrelfish
Sargocentron spiniferum

Its body is moderately compressed and tall; the snout is pointed with relatively large eyes. The dorsal fin is well developed with red interradial membranes. Coloring of the body is red with spots of the same color, but darker on the opercula and at the base of the pectoral fins. This is a nocturnal species, and has territorial habits. It measures up to forty-five centimeters in legth.

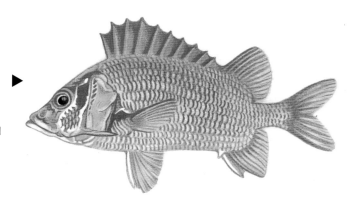

PLATYCEPHALIDAE FAMILY

Crocodile fish
Cociella crocodila

The body is compressed toward the front and is slightly cylindrical towards the rear; it is covered with rough scales. The mouth is large and is well lined with small, sharp teeth. There are two dorsal fins, the first of which is preceded by an isolated spine. The caudal fin is rounded. The coloring ranges from brownish to olive-gray, with dark spots on the back. Normally, it can be found on the seabed or partly buried in silt, by itself or in pairs. It grows to be sixty to seventy centimeters in length.

SCORPAENIDAE FAMILY

Clearfin turkeyfish
Pterois radiata

◄ Oblong body with a large head and a large mouth. The rays of the pectoral fins are very long, do not branch out, and the upper ones are joined by a membrane but only at the base. All of the rays are poisonous. The body is a brownish red with white stripes. Above the eyes there are long fleshy papillae. It can attain a size of 25 centimeters.

Turkeyfish
Pterois volitans

Body is similar to the previous species. The coloring presents broad brown vertical stripes; not all the same width. The rays of the fins are not naked, but possess a more or less developed membrane that makes them similar to feathers. The odd-numbered fins bear rows of brownish-black spots. Around the mouth and above the eyes one can clearly see some indented appendages. It can attain a size of 35 centimeters.

►

Devil scorpionfish
Scorpaenopsis diabolus

◄ A slightly oval body, massive and high, with numerous fleshy excrescences. The head is large and is covered with spines; the mouth is wide and turns upwards. The pectoral fins extend to the anal fin. The coloring provides excellent camouflage, as this is a species that hunts from ambush. The tailfin has broad dark vertical stripes. The spines of the dorsal fin are poisonous, but not to the same degree as those of the stonefish. It grows to a length of thirty centimeters.

Stonefish
Synanceia verrucosa

A moderately oblong body, compressed at the sides and free of scales. The head is massive, covered with crests and spines, and the eyes - which are perhaps the most noticeable part - are turned upwards, as is the wide mouth. The pectoral fins are very well developed. The coloring provides excellent camouflage, and the fish is virtually identical to a stone that is practically invisible. The glands at the base of the spines produce a very powerful poison, which can be fatal.

►

SERRANIDAE FAMILY

Scalefin anthias
Pseudanthias squamipinnis

◄ Oval, compressed body, which ends in a sickle-shaped tail with elongated lobes. The snout is short and rounded, and the mouth is terminal. The dorsal fin is well developed, especially in the male, which has several particularly long fore rays. The coloring is reddish, with red spots near the pectoral fins. The females have yellowish shadings. This fish is gregarious, and forms schools dominated by one or two males. They attain a length of fifteen to seventeen centimeters

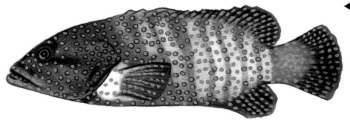

Coral grouper
Cephalopholis miniata

The body is similar to that of *Cephalopholis argus*. The rear edges of the dorsal and anal fins are less rounded than in the previous species. The coloring is a very bright reddish-orange, with numerous small dark-blue ocellate spots scattered all over the body and fins, and tends to become darker in the adults. A fairly territorial species, it prefers to remain in the general vicinity of grottoes and underwater crannies. According to some observations, this fish tends to become gregarious during the mating season, and to gather to restrict areas. It attains a length of forty to forty-five centimeters.

Peacock grouper
Cephalopholis argus

◀ The body is massive, tapered, and slightly compressed. The head is powerful, with a slightly prominent lower jaw. The edge of the caudal fin is rounded. The dorsal fin has nine spinous rays and a rounded rear edge that ends in proximity of the caudal peduncle and opposite the anal fin. The coloring is marked by numerous dark blue spots and by ten dark bands on the sides. The fins are dark blue. These fish attain a length of fifty centimeters.

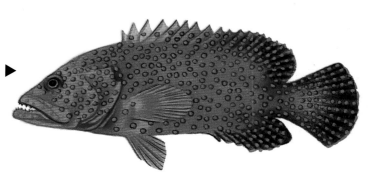

Lunartail grouper
Variola louti

Tapered body which terminates toward the rear with a tall caudal peduncle supporting an unmistakable tail in the form of a crescent moon or sickle, and with elongated lobes. Dorsal and anal fins have pointed rear edges. The coloring is reddish or brownish, with purple highlights and numerous pale spots. This is a fairly common species and attains lengths of up to eighty or eighty-five centimeters.

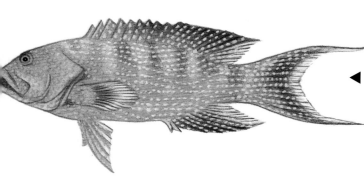

Potato cod
Epinephelus tukula

The body is broad and powerful. The head is tapered, with a convex intraorbital space. The snout is elongated and the mouth is wide. The lower jaw is more developed than the upper. The coloring is grayish-brown, with large, pronounced dark spots arrayed along the sides and on the tail. The fins are marked by smaller but numerous spots. This one is among the largest groupers, and can grow to be as long as two meters.

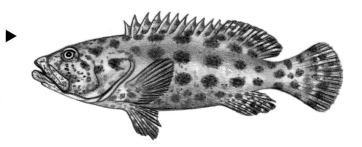

Giant grouper
Epinephelus tauvina

◀ Tapered body, slightly compressed, but not as tall as other groupers. The snout is pointed, and the mouth is broad and terminal. The caudal fin is rounded. The dorsal fin is not very tall, and has eleven spinous rays. Along the back, at the base of the dorsal fin, it is possible to detect a number of large dark spots. Smaller spots are scattered along the entire body, whose coloring is basically very pale. This species can grow to be longer than two meters.

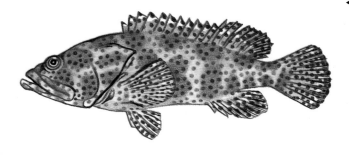

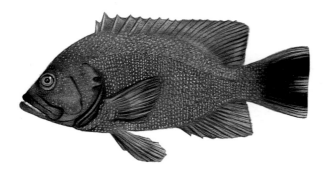

Redmouth grouper
Aethaloperca rogaa

Grouper with stout, tall, compressed shape. The head is large and the dorsal profile appears to be concave, in line with the eyes. The mouth is large and the lips are thick. Adults of this species have a sort of hump. The dorsal, anal, and caudal fins have a straight rear edge. The coloration is uniformly dark brown. The mouth and the opercula appear to be reddish. In the young of this species, the tail has a white edging. These fish live on other fish, and live along the reef. They grow to be sixty centimeters in length.

GRAMMISTIDAE FAMILY

Goldstriped goldfish
Grammistes sexlineatus

The body is oval, tall, and compressed, and is covered with many small scales. The mouth is wide, and the lower jaw bears a small fleshy excrescence. This species is easily recognized by its distinctive pattern of whitish-yellow stripes running lengthwise from the head to the caudal peduncle; these stripes are extremely noticeable on the dark brown and blue of the body. If this fish is alarmed, it secretes a mucus that is toxic to other fish. It grows to be thirty centimeters in length.

PSEUDOCHROMIDAE FAMILY

Sunrise dottyback
Pseudochromis flavivertex

The body is elongated, compressed, and is distinguished by a very long dorsal fin and a long anal fin. The eyes are in a subdorsal position and protrude slightly. The two-tone coloring is distinctive; it is a bright chrome yellow above, while the rest of the body is light blue. It lives by preference among the branches of coral, near a sandy bottom. This fish grows to be ten centimeters in length.

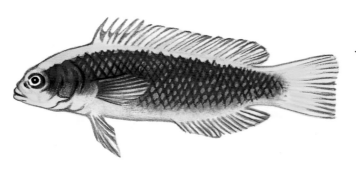

Olive dottyback
Pseudochromis fridmani

This species is only found in the Red Sea. The body is elongated and tapered toward the front. The snout is short, with large eyes and a terminal mouth. The caudal fin, which is truncated in the young, tends to have a slightly more elongated lower lobe in the adults of the species. This fish has a bright purple coloring, and is almost luminescent. A thin dark band runs from the tip of the snout to the eye. The opercula have a fairly pronounced dark blue spot. The upper lobe of the caudal fin is practically transparent. This species is often found under coral umbrellas that jut from the walls of the reef. They grow to be six to seven centimeters in length.

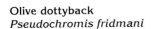

CIRRHITIDAE FAMILY

Longnose hawkfish
Oxycirrhites typus

The body is slightly cylindrical, taller at the center, and terminates in an elongated snout. The mouth is small. The spinous part of the dorsal fin bears a series of appendages. Pectoral fins are particularly well developed, and this fish uses them to balance upon gorgonians. Here the fish is perfectly camouflaged, due to a series of red stripes that form a checkerboard on its body. It attains a length of between ten and thirteen centimeters.

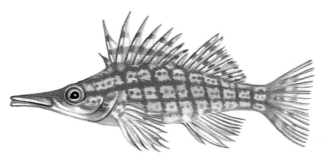

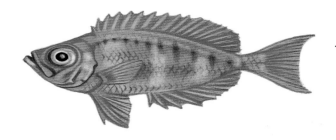

ECHENEIDAE FAMILY

Sharksucker
Echeneis naucrates

Elongated body with a head that is flattened dorsally, where the suction cup is found that is typical of remoras, and which is nothing more than a modified dorsal fin. The mouth features a well developed lower jaw. The dorsal and anal fins are similar and symmetrical. The coloring is dark gray or brownish with a darker band running lengthwise. The edges of the fins are whitish. This species attains a length of about a meter.

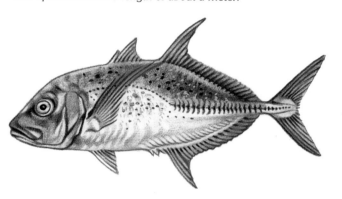

Bigeye Trevally
Caranx sexfasciatus

The body is elongated and compressed; the forward silhouette is rounded. The lower jaw tends to jut. On the caudal stalk, there are evident keels; the caudal fin is sharply forked. The coloring is blue-gray or blue-green on the back. The lobes of the caudal fin show a blackish hue. The sides are greenish-yellow or silvery. The young of the species are golden yellow, with four to seven broad dark vertical bands. This fish grows to be longer than a meter and a half.

PRIACANTHIDAE FAMILY

Goggle eye
Priacanthus hamrur

The body is oval, tall, and compressed. The snout is short, and the large eyes stand out, revealing the nocturnal habits of the species. The mouth is turned upward. The caudal fin is shaped like a crescent moon, with elongated lobes, especially in the adults of the species. The coloring is generally a dark reddish hue, but can change rapidly, acquiring more or less pronounced silvery highlights or becoming striped with red on silvery body. The dorsal and anal fins have dark highlights along their edges. This fish attains a length of forty to forty-five centimeters.

CARANGIDAE FAMILY

Bluefin Trevally
Caranx melampygus

The body is elongated, and rather tall; forward, it terminates with a convex head and a high forehead. The eyes are small. The caudal peduncle is narrow and reinforced with visible bony plates, the lateral line is complete and arched anteriorly. The coloring is greenish-brown, with numerous small black spots. The long, sickle-shaped pectoral fins with scales on their sides are yellow in the young of the species. This fish grows to be longer than one meter.

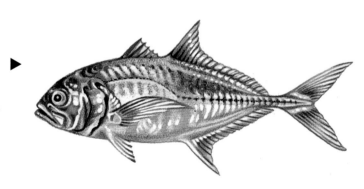

LETHRINIDAE FAMILY

Spangled emperor
Lethrinus nebulosus

The body is fairly tall and compressed. The head is elongated with a sharply oblique forward profile. The snout is pointed. The eyes tend upwards. The mouth is entirely red. The dorsal fin is well developed; the pectoral fins have scales on the inner section. The basic coloring, gray and uniform, is enlivened by light blue stripes and spots, more evident on the sides, on the opercula, and behind the eyes. Present in large numbers on open and shallow seabeds. It may measure seventy-five centimeters or more in length.

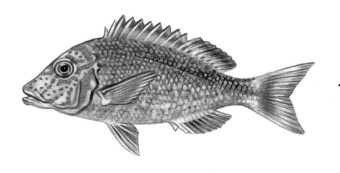

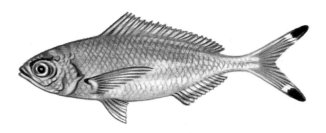

CAESIONIDAE FAMILY

Suez fusilier
Caesio suevicus

◀ The rounded and tapered body is rather elongated. The mouth is small and has thin teeth in front of a row of very small teeth. The upper jaw can be extended forward quite easily while capturing the small prey upon which the species feeds. Particularly distinctive is the forked caudal fin. The coloring is generally silvery, with yellow nuances; the lobes of the tailfin are black. These fish travel in numerous schools. They measure fifteen to twenty centimeters in length.

HAEMULIDAE FAMILY

Blackspotted grunt
Plectorhynchus gaterinus

The body is tapered, tall and slightly compressed. The head is well developed, the snout is short and convex. The eyes are large. The mouth is not very large and distinguished by a pair of thick lips. The adults are unmistakable, and have a basic coloring of bright yellow, upon which numerous black spots stand out. The young fish, instead, have five black longitudinal bands; the two bands closest to the back extend all the way back to the caudal fin. During daytime, this species tends to form schools close to the reef's slope. It measures up to fifty centimeters.

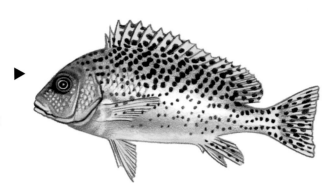

LUTJANIDAE FAMILY

Twinspot snapper
Lutjanus bohar

◀ Elongated, tall, powerful body. The snout is pointed, and the mouth is wide and lined with one row of conical teeth above and below, and there are pronounced front canine teeth. The fins are well developed. There is only one dorsal fin; the sickle-shaped pectoral fins stretch almost all the way to where the anal fin is attached. The coloring is a reddish-purple, darker on the back, and with yellowish highlights on either side of the head. The fins are dark, and are partly edged with white. The spinous rays of the dorsal fin are white at the tips. This fish attains a length of seventy to seventy-five centimeters.

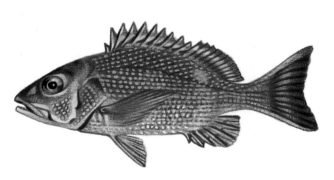

Bluestriped snapper
Lutjanus kasmira

Tapered body with pointed snout. Large eyes and mouth. The dorsal fin extends to the height of the caudal peduncle. The coloring is golden yellow on the back, becoming gradually paler along the sides and almost silvery on the belly. Typical of the species are the four light stripes running lengthwise; the longest of the stripes runs from the mouth to the caudal peduncle. The edges of the dorsal and the caudal fins are black. This fish measures forty centimeters in length.

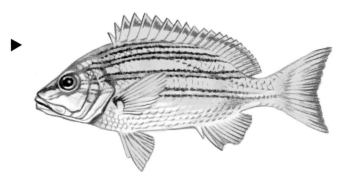

MULLIDAE FAMILY

Yellowsaddle goatfish
Parupeneus cyclostomus

◀ The high, tapered body ends in a jutting snout. The lower jaw is distinguished by the presence of two long barbels that extend back to the ventral fins. The two dorsal fins are sharply separated. The tail is typically two-lobed. The head has bluish stripes that are fairly evident. The second dorsal fin has a dark spot toward the rear. The coloring is brighter in the young. It measures thirty-five centimeters in length.

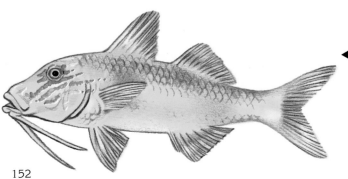

Forsskal's goatfish
Parupeneus forsskali

The shape of the body is typical of the genus *Parupeneus*. The barbels, which are still present, are however far smaller than those found in the previous species described. The coloring is a silvery blue with yellow nuances on the back. The caudal peduncle is bright yellow with a pronounced dark spot at the center. Along the sides there is a dark band which covers the eye.

PEMPHERIDAE FAMILY

Vanikoro sweeper
Pempheris vanicolensis

The body is oblong and compressed, taller toward the front and tapered toward the rear. The dorsal silhouette is nearly a straight line, while the ventral profile is concave around the long anal fin. The tail is slightly incised. The mouth is wide, oblique, and terminal. The eyes are large. This species is nocturnal, and forms numerous schools in the shelter of coral reefs. The coloring is light, pink and translucent. It measures twelve to fifteen centimeters in length.

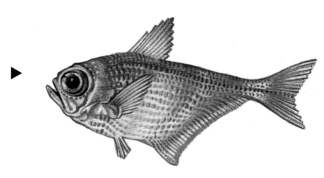

EPHIPPIDAE FAMILY

Batfish
Platax orbicularis

The unmistakably shaped body is tall, compressed, and discoid, with anal and dorsal fins that are symmetrical and well developed. Narrower in the young, these fins tend to broaden and become more rounded in adults. The mouth and the eyes are small. The coloring is distinguished by broad dark vertical bands along the sides, which tend to disappear with age. They live in schools. They measure fifty centimeters in length.

CHAETODONTIDAE FAMILY

Threadfin butterflyfish
Chaetodon auriga

The body is nearly rectangular, very tall and compressed. The head is concave toward the front, and terminates in a pointed, short snout. A broad dark band covers the eye, narrowing on the back. The dorsal fin features a dark ocellate spot along the rearmost edge, topped by a number of elongated and filamentous rays which constitute one of the distinctive features of this species. The *Chaetodon auriga* swims alone or in pairs. It measures twenty to twenty-five centimeters in length.

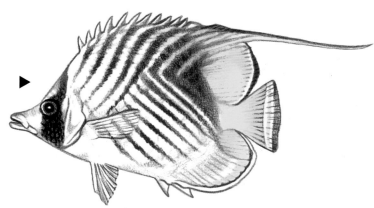

Exquisite butterflyfish
Chaetodon austriacus

The body is typically oval and compressed. The snout is short. The dorsal fin is very long. The anal fin is well developed. The rear edges of the fins just mentioned seem to shade into the caudal fin. The background coloring is yellow. Along the sides, there is a series of slightly diagonal stripes of a blue-black color. The snout is dark and a vertical black stripe entirely covers the eye. The anal fin, the caudal fin, and the rear edge of the dorsal fin are black. This species feeds entirely on polyps. This fish measures twelve centimeters in length.

Striped butterflyfish
Chaetodon fasciatus

The shape of the body is similar to that of *Chaetodon austriacus*. The background coloring is yellow. Along the sides, nine or ten slightly diagonal bands of a dark color stand out, and merge into a single band of the same color parallel to the dorsal fin. The dorsal, caudal, and anal fins are trimmed with a brownish-yellow band. The black eye band is followed by shorter white band. It measures eighteen centimeters in length.

Blackback butterflyfish
Chaetodon melannotus

The body appears nearly oval, tall and compressed. The head has an oblique and slightly concave forward profile. The snout is short and pointed. The most distinctive feature of this species is the black band that vertically cuts across the snout, covering the eye. The rear portion of the caudal peduncle and forward portion of the anal fin have black spots. All of the fins are yellow. On the sides of this fish there are diagonal rows of points that converge in a dark dorsal band. These fish attain a length of eighteen centimeters.

Paleface butterflyfish
Chaetodon mesoleucos

A slightly square body, extremely compressed laterally, and tall. The forward profile is convex. The snout is short. The forward portion is white and the rear portion is brown, with twelve black vertical stripes. The caudal fin is black and is trimmed in white, with a whitish, orange-tipped crescent. The upper silhouette of the snout is marked by a black band that covers the eyes. It measures fourteen to sixteen centimeters in length.

Crown butterflyfish
Chaetodon paucifasciatus

The body is tall and compressed. The snout is pointed. The background color is quite pale. The forward section is whitish with a strip of tawny reddish-yellow covering the eye. On the sides are four or five bands of black diamond shapes. On the rear part of the body there is a distinctive red spot. A band of red distinguishes the caudal fin. In young specimens, at the center of the red spot there is an ocellar dot. This fish generally swims in pairs or in small groups near the underwater meadows. It measures fourteen centimeters in length.

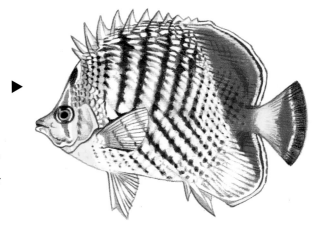

Masked butterflyfish
Chaetodon semilarvatus

◀ The species is peculiar to the Red Sea. The shape is almost discoid, with a small prominent snout. The colouring is almost uniformly orange-yellow with fine dark diagonal stripes. The eye is surrounded by a dark bluish spot that extends as far as to the operculum. A dark narrow line underscores the outline of the dorsal and anal fins. The pectoral fins are transparent; the ventral fins are yellow. These fish are often found in schools. They grow to be eighteen to twenty centimeters in length.

Pennantfish
Heniochus intermedius

The body is tall, disk-shaped, and extremely compressed. The head is small, the snout is slightly elongated. The forward portion of the body is distinguished by a broad black band that covers the eye and the operculum and extends to the base of the dorsal fin. A second band runs diagonally along the rear portion of the body, starting from the caudal peduncle. The spinous ray of the dorsal fin is prominent as a banner. This fish measures twenty-five centimeters in length.

POMACANTHIDAE FAMILY

Emperor angelfish
Pomacanthus imperator

◀ The shape of the body is nearly oval, with a practically rectilinear forward profile of the head. The snout is very short. The dorsal and anal fins have a rounded forward edge that just exceeds the caudal stalk. The young of this species are dark blue with lighter concentric bands, the last of which forms a closed circle on the caudal stalk. Adults feature many diagonal yellow bands. The eyes are masked by a black stripe edged in light blue, followed by a similar stripe on the operculum. This fish grows to a length of thirty-five centimeters.

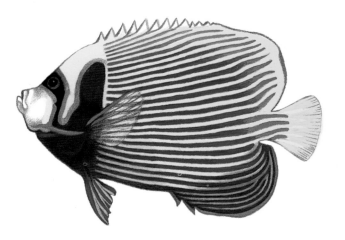

Arabian angelfish
Pomacanthus asfur

The body is tall and compressed. The head has a convex forward profile which ends in a short snout. The lower jaw is slightly prominent. The dorsal and anal fins are well developed, and their rays extend far backwards, long past the rear margin of the caudal fin. The coloring of the young, with vertical whitish-yellow stripes, becomes a uniform dark blue in adults, which can be distinguished by the yellow spot on the sides, which extends to part of the back and the tail in the same color. This fish has a length of thirty or thirty-five centimeters.

155

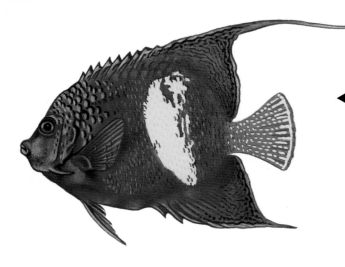

Yellowbar angelfish
Pomacanthus maculosus

The shape of the body is quite similar to that of *Pomacanthus asfur*. The young of the species have light vertical stripes on the sides, and can be distinguished from the young of *Pomacanthus asfur* because their caudal fins are light in color and translucent. The adult features a large yellow spot on their side, which however does not extend to the dorsal area of the base of the dorsal fin. These fish tend to be solitary, and grow to a length of thirty centimeters.

Royal angelfish
Pygoplites diacanthus

The body is less tall than usual in angelfish. The rear edges of the dorsal and anal fins are well developed, but do not exceed the caudal fin. The body has a background coloring of orange yellow, with eight or nine dark blue bands. The eyes are surrounded by two sharply defined dark blue stripes. The dorsal fin has a fairly dark vermiculation, while the anal fin has parallel yellow stripes along the edge of the fin. The young of this species are fairly similar, and have a posterior ocellar spot. This fish grows to a length of twenty-five or thirty centimeters.

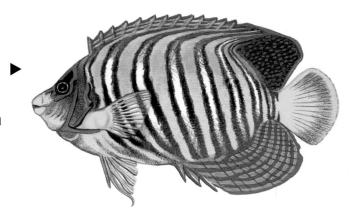

POMACENTRIDAE FAMILY

Sergeant major
Abudefduf saxatilis

Configuration of the body is similar to the other described species. The grayish silvery coloring shifts toward bright yellow on the back. Along the sides of the fish, there are five dark vertical bands, the first of which intersects the rearmost edge of the operculum. The coloring becomes lighter when the fish lives near sandy seabeds, and darker near coral. Adult males acquire bluish and purplish nuances when they are guarding the spawn. They attain a length of ten to fifteen centimeters.

Twobar anemonefish
Amphiprion bicinctus

The body is oval and rounded. The snout is short and stubby, with a small mouth. The dorsal fin extends along much of the dorsum and presents a slight saddle formation which separates the spinous portion from the part with soft rays. The caudal fin has two lobes. The background coloring ranges from orange to brownish orange, with two white vertical strips. The younger specimens may have a third stripe on the stalk of the tailfin. It generally tends to live in symbiosis with anemonefish of the genus *Heteractis*. It attains a length of thirteen to fifteen centimeters.

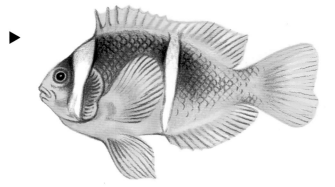

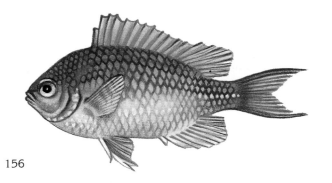

Bluegreen chromis
Chromis viridis

The shape of the body is roughly similar to the damselfish of the Mediterranean. The coloring tends to bluish, and is relatively intense, with slight nuances along the edge of the scales. This fish is gregarious, and tends to form large groups, each of which seems to colonize a specific coral formation, favoring those near the sheer walls at the outer edge of the reef. They measure from eight to ten centimeters in length.

Half-and-half chromis
Chromis dimidiata

The shape of the body is similar to the species described immediately above. The coloring, however, is radically different, and allows one to recognize this species quite easily; half the body is white and half is dark brown or black. This fish is gregarious, and tends to form huge schools near large coral formations, venturing to greater depths than the *Chromis viridis*. It measures seven centimeters in length.

Banded dascyllus
Dascyllus aruanus

The body is fairly stubby, squarish, tall, and compressed. The mouth is small with a slightly prominent lower jaw. The background coloring is whitish, with three distinctive diagonal dark bands, the first of which covers the eye and the mouth. This fish forms small groups, each of which is closely associated with a single coral colony. Only larger specimens venture at any distance from the corals, while smaller ones remain in permanent residence among the branches. They measure eight to ten centimeters in length.

Domino damselfish
Dascyllus trimaculatus

The shape of the body is typical of the genus. The mouth is small, considering that this is a fish feeding on plankton. The coloring is the most distinctive feature, and quite sufficient to make the fish unmistakable. In fact, this species is either completely black or dark brown, with three white spots: one on either side and a third on the forehead. These spots are most pronounced in the young, and tend to fade in adulthood. The species is quite common around anemonefish, amidst long-spined black urchins *(Diadema antillarum)*, and amidst *Acropora* corals. It measures up to fourteen centimeters in length.

LABRIDAE FAMILY

Yellowtail wrasse
Anampses meleagrides

Tapered body, with a generally oval silhouette, and with a slight frontal hump, more pronounced in females. The mouth is terminal, and protractile, with large fleshy lips. The coloring of adult males is dark and purplish with more-or-less elongated bluish spots along the edge of the scales. Dorsal and anal fins feature bluish stripes, as does the rearmost edge of the caudal fin, the lobes of which are elongated. Females have a dark coloring, spangled with numerous white spots. The snout and the lower head are reddish. The caudal fin is yellow. This fish measures up to twenty-five centimeters in length.

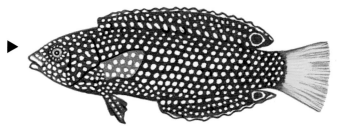

Abudjubbe wrasse
Cheilinus abudjubbe

A member of the *Labridae* family with a particularly powerful structure, with a tall body covered with large scales. The head is elongated and convex; the mouth is well developed with pronounced canine-shaped teeth. The background coloring is dark, especially along the side, where a number of red spots can be seen. Distinctive red stripes are arrayed around the eyes. The fins are lighter in color and distinguished by yellow-greenish spots, distributed in rows along the rays. This fish often feeds on sea urchins. It measures thirty-five centimeters in length.

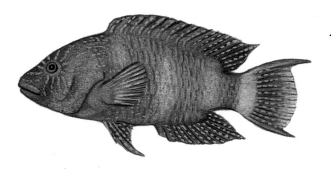

Broomtail wrasse
Cheilinus lunulatus

The body is compressed and tall, with large scales. The head is convex and stubby with a short tail. The mouth is large and protractile. Males have a relatively dark background coloring, especially on the head, and feature purple stripes that are sometimes particularly pronounced along the edges of the scales. The pectoral fins are yellow. Bluish nuances distinguish the mouth and fins. The caudal fin is distinguished by a fringed rear edge that is peculiar to the species. This fish measures up to fifty centimeters in length.

Humphead wrasse
Cheilinus undulatus

The humphead wrasse is the largest known member of the *Labridae* family, and has a very distinctive tall and stubby structure. The mouth is large and features thick protractile lips which allow this fish literally to suck up its prey. In the adults, the head is marked by a pronounced bump on the forehead. The greenish-gray coloring has irregular greenish-yellow stripes along the sides, shifting to orange on the head. These fish can be as long as two meters, and can weigh more than 170-180 kilograms.

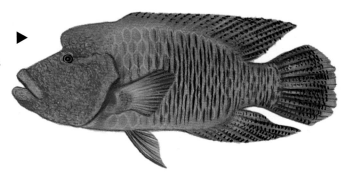

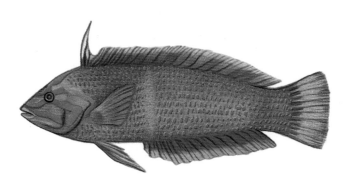

African coris
Coris africana

Tapered, slender body, with a silhouette reminding one of the Mediterranean rainbow wrasse. The first two rays on the dorsal fin are generally elongated, in adult specimens. The reddish coloring features fine greenish stripes at the base of each scale. The head is greenish and has broad greenish bands, the widest of which runs from the rear edge of the mouth to the operculum. Males have a green stripe along the side, just above the point of origin of the anal fin. This fish reaches a length of thirty-five to forty centimeters.

Red Sea bird wrasse
Gomphosus caeruleus

A typically oval body, slightly compressed. The snout is distinctively elongated and tubular in the adults. The mouth is terminal, but sufficiently well developed to prey on small animals. The caudal fin is rounded, but tends to develop elongated lobes with time. The coloring is dark blue in males. Females are green on their backs and yellowish on their bellies, with black spots on their sides. They measure from twenty to twenty-five centimeters in length.

Cleaner wrasse
Labroides dimidiatus

The body is compressed, elongated, and covered with large scales. The head is pointy; the snout is elongated, with a small terminal mouth lined with numerous small and pointed teeth. The upper jaw is longer than the lower. The forward half of the body is brownish, and darker on the back than on the belly. A broad black band runs from the beginning of the snout all the way to the tip of the caudal fin, widening as it goes. The base of the anal fin and the rear part of the body are an intense dark blue. It attains a length of ten centimeters.

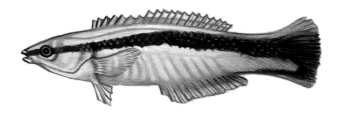

Moon wrasse
Thalassoma lunare

The body is tapered, powerful, and slightly compressed. The head is rounded, the snout is short. The mouth is small and the lips are thin. The caudal fin is truncated in the young; partially moon-shaped in adults, especially larger males, which are also bluish. The coloring is greenish with vertical purplish-red stripes on the sides. The head is greenish-blue with broad pink bands running roughly lengthwise. The caudal fin is yellowish at the center with pink stripes along the lobes. It attains a length of twenty-five to thirty centimeters.

SCARIDAE FAMILY

Rusty parrotfish
Scarus ferrugineus

The body is tapered, slightly compressed at the sides, and covered with large scales. The head is large and the mouth is in a terminal position. The upper jaw is slightly prominent. One distinctive feature is the large teeth of the jaws, which join together so as to form a beak of four plates. The male, which has a greenish snout and fins edged in blue-green, is more colorful than the female. This fish prefers a protected coral seabed. It attains a length of forty centimeters.

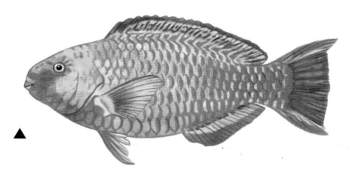

Steephead parrotfish
Scarus gibbus

The body is oval, tall, and powerful. The head has a forward silhouette that is quite convex, and nearly vertical. The dental plates are not particularly pronounced. On the cheeks, are three rows of large scales. The caudal fin is semilunar. The coloring is brownish yellow, while the lower part of the snout is green in the females. On the scales, are fairly intense pink stripes. These remain in males as well; males have on their dorsal area a greenish coloring with touches of violet. The ventral section is blue-green. The rear of the caudal fin has a green edge. It attains a length of seventy centimeters.

Bumphead parrotfish
Bolbometopon muricatum

The body is powerful, tall compressed at the sides, and covered with large scales. At the sides of the snout and near the mouth there are three rows of scales. The coloring is greenish-blue both in males and females. The snout and the gullet are pink as is the forward portion of the prominence of the males, which can be thus easily recognized. The young of this species are dark brown, with a double row of white spots along the upper half of the body. They grow to be one and a half meters long.

BLENNIIDAE FAMILY

Mimic blenny
Aspidontus taeniatus

The body is elongated and tapered. Its shape and coloring mimic the *Labroides dimidiatus*. Distinguishing between the two species is not simple, even for other fish, which are often thereby deceived by the mimic blenny. The most evidently distinguishing feature is the shape of the snout and of the mouth, which turn downward due to the greater development of the upper jaw. The black band running lengthwise is less developed. It measures twelve to thirteen centimeters.

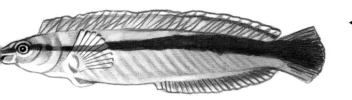

159

SPHYRAENIDAE FAMILY

Blackfin barracuda
Sphyraena qenie

The body is elongated and is typical of the barracuda. The lower jaw, devoid of any fleshy excrescence, is prominent, but the back of the jaw goes no further back than the forward margin of the eye. The first dorsal fin begins after the pectoral fins. The second dorsal fin is symmetrical with the anal fin. The caudal fin is forked, and strangely can have three lobes in the larger specimens. The coloring is silvery, with eighteen to twenty-two dark vertical bands. The dorsal and caudal fins are dark, as is the anal fin, while the last two anal rays are white. This species grows to over a meter in length.

GOBIIDAE FAMILY

Sixspot goby
Valenciennea sexguttata

The tapered body is covered with small rough scales; the snout is pointed and the mouth is turned slightly upward, lined with a great many teeth some of which are quite large. There are two dorsal fins; the first dorsal fin is marked by small round or oblong dark blue spots. Along this fish's sides are one or two barely visible stripes, which do not reach the caudal fin. It lives part of the time buried in sandy seabeds. This fish grows to a length of thirteen centimeters.

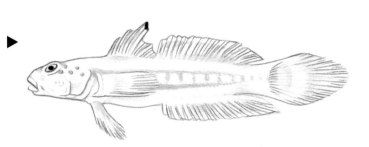

ACANTHURIDAE FAMILY

Black surgeonfish
Acanthurus gahham

The body is oval, tall and slightly compressed. The forward profile is rounded. The dorsal and anal fins are well developed. The caudal fin, distinguished by a white band at its base, is sickle-shaped, with the upper and lower lobes elongated. A short black band can be seen behind the eyes alongside the spines of the caudal peduncle. The pectoral fins have a dark yellow border. This fish grows to a length of forty centimeters.

Brown surgeonfish
Acanthurus nigrofuscus

The body is oval, tall and compressed. The forward profile is extremely convex. The snout is dark brown or purplish-brown, with or without thin bluish-gray lines running lengthwise along the side. The lips are black. The rear edges of the anal and dorsal fins are distinguished by a black spot. The head and chin have numerous orange spots. The spine on the peduncle is bordered in black. This fish grows to a length of twenty centimeters.

Sohal surgeonfish
Acanthurus sohal

The body is oval, tall, and compressed. The head is powerful and rounded. The mouth is distinguished by thick lips and spatulate teeth suited to grazing on algae, on which this fish feeds. The coloring is bluish-gray, with numerous dark stripes along the side and the upper part of the head. The cheeks are white. The fins are dark and edged with a light-blue band. The fearsome spines on the caudal peduncle are distinguished by their bright orange color. This fish behaves in a territorial manner, and attains a length of forty centimeters.

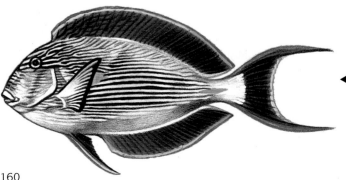

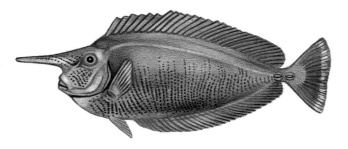

Spotted unicornfish
Naso brevirostris

◀ This is the most distinctive of the surgeonfish, easily recognized for its powerful oval body that terminates in a long beak, which in turn extends well beyond the snout. On the sides of the peduncle there are two bony plates which each bear a sharp spine. The caudal fin is rounded. The coloring ranges from grayish-blue to olive brown. The lips are sometimes bluish. The tail features a pale band along the lower edge. This fish has gregarious habits, and attains a length of fifty centimeters.

Orangespine unicornfish
Naso lituratus

The body is oval, compressed, and tall toward the front. The head is powerful with a dorsal profile that forms a forty-five degree angle. The snout is pointed; the mouth is small and is lined with sharp teeth with rounded tips. On the sides of the peduncle are two bony plates, each bearing a sharp spine which curves forward. The caudal fin is semilunar, with pointed lobes and long filamentous rays. The coloring is yellowish-brown. The caudal peduncle is orange. Between the eyes is a light yellow spot. The dorsal fin is yellowish-orange, black at the base, with a white edge. This fish attains a length of forty-five centimeters.

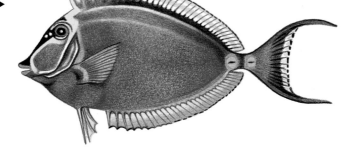 ▶

Bluespine unicornfish
Naso unicornis

The body is oval and elongate, tall and compressed. The forward profile is marked by a beak that is not long enough to exceed the mouth. The snout is pointed; the mouth is ◀ terminal, with powerful compressed teeth. On the sides of the caudal peduncle are two bluish spines shaped like chisels, which are not movable, but attached to bony plates. The coloring is light gray, and olive. In some cases the lips are blue and the dorsal and anal fins have orange stripes. The caudal fin is crescent-shaped with elongated, filmentous lobes. This fish attains a length of fifty to sixty centimeters.

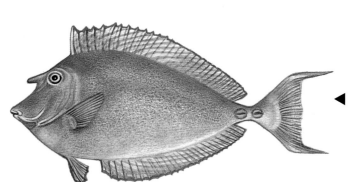

Yellowtail surgeonfish
Zebrasoma xanthurum

The body is compressed laterally and covered with small scales. The forward portion of the silhouette of the snout is typically concave. The mouth is small, terminal and protractile. The single dorsal fin is well developed, rounded to the rear, and almost symmetrical to the anal fin. The spines on the caudal peduncle can vary in size. The coloring is dark blue, with small reddish spots on the head, which tend to follow a straight-line array behind the eyes, ending at the pectoral fin. The caudal fin and the edge of the pectoral fins are bright yellow. This fish grows to a length of forty centimeters.

▶

SIGANIDAE FAMILY

Stellate rabbitfish
Siganus stellatus

Oval, compressed body, covered with very small scales. The snout is slightly pointed; the mouth is terminal and is lined with numerous small teeth. The cheeks are covered with large scales. The coloring is generally a grayish-green spangled with small brown spots that tend to become smaller toward the back of the head, where they form a green oval shade at the base of the spines of the dorsal fin. Large black spots are present along the lateral line. This fish grows to a length of forty centimeters.

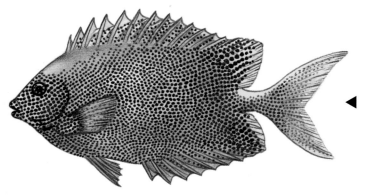 ◀

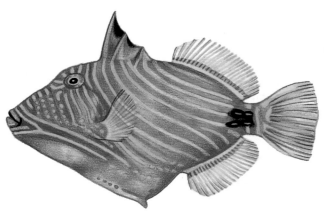

 **Orangestriped triggerfish**
Balistapus undulatus

A slightly oval body, tall and compressed, covered with small bony plates. The head is very well developed and measures roughly a third of the length of the body. The eyes are quite far along the side of the fish. The mouth is terminal, and is distinguished by powerful jaws lined with massive teeth. The background coloring is dark, and orange-yellow stripes stand out on it. Bands of the same color surround the mouth. The dorsal and anal fins are light blue. The caudal fin is yellow. This fish grows to a length of seventy centimeters.

Titan triggerfish
Balistoides viridescens

The shape of the body is typical of the family. The mouth is terminal. There is a deep depression between the eyes. On the stalk of the caudal fin are two to four rows, running lengthwise, of large tubercles. The coloring is greenish; the edges of the fins are black. A black band runs around the upper jaw. The stalk of the caudal fin is fairly light in color. This species is aggressive, especially during the mating season. This fish grows to a length of seventy to seventy-five centimeters.

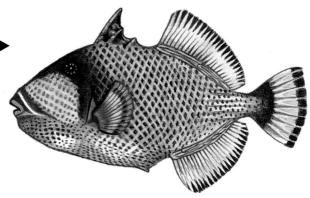

Redtooth triggerfish
Odonus niger

The body is slightly oval. The head is pointed. The mouth is terminal, and the lower jaw is more developed than the upper. The coloring of the body is blue-black while the head is greenish with blueish stripes leading from the mouth. The caudal fin is semilunar, and the lobes are well developed and quite long. This fish tends to gather in small groups, and grows to a length of fifty centimeters.

Blue yellow spotted
Pseudobalistes fuscus

The shape of the body is typical of the family. The head is rounded. There are large scales under the opercula. Along the lower portion of the snout there are horizontal channels. The coloring is dark brown with yellow or orange spots on the scales. The edge of the fins is yellowish. The caudal fin is rounded in the young and has elongated lobes in adults. This fish grows to a length of fifty to fifty-five centimeters.

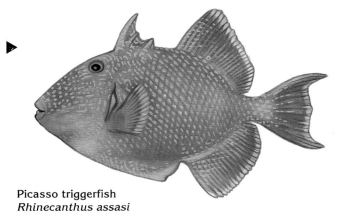

Picasso triggerfish
Rhinecanthus assasi

The body is oval and the head triangular, the snout is pointed and the mouth is terminal. On the stalk of the caudal fin, there are three rows of small spines. The lips are yellowish and a stripe of the same color extends from the mouth to the operculum. A black vertical band covers the eyes. On the sides are diagonal stripes. The caudal fin is slightly rounded. This fish grows to a length of twenty-five to thirty centimeters.

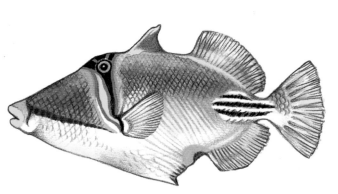

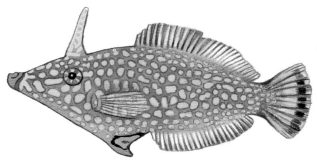

OSTRACIIDAE FAMILY

Cube boxfish
Ostracion cubicus

The body is shaped like a box, rectangular with rounded off angles and corners, and has no spines. The dorsal and anal fins are small, but are driven by powerful muscles which the fish uses for locomotion. The ventral and caudal fins are more developed; the caudal serves as a rudder. Males have a uniform violet coloring. The young of the species are yellow with black spots. This fish grows to a length of forty-five centimeters.

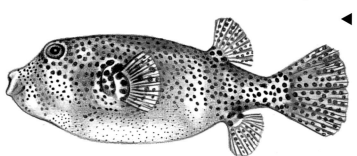

Pearl toby pufferfish
Canthigaster margaritata

This is a blowfish with slightly compressed head and body dotted with small spines which become pronounced when the fish swells up. The snout is elongated and the mouth is protractile. The caudal fin is truncated. At the center of the back and the belly there is a fold of skin which can erect. The coloring is dark yellow on the back, and shades off on the belly. The body is dotted with dark blue spots edged in black. Around the eyes there are radial stripes, of the same color as the ocellar spots. At the base of the dorsal fin, are two dark blue stripes. This fish grows to a length of twelve or thirteen centimeters.

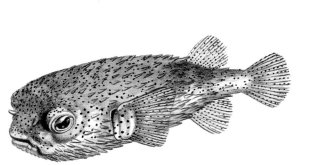

MONACANTHIDAE FAMILY

◀ Harlequin filefish
Oxymonacanthus halli

The body is oval and compressed, and is covered with a rough epidermis, due to the presence of minuscule denticles. The snout is typically elongated and tubular, with a lower jaw that is more developed than the upper. The background coloring is green, with a regular pattern of large bright yellow or orange spots. It forms small groups near branches of *Acropora* corals, on the polyps of which it feeds. This fish grows to a length of ten or twelve centimeters.

▶

TETRADONTIDAE FAMILY

◀ Blackspotted pufferfish
Arothron stellatus

The body is elongated and globular, with an oval silhouette, and is covered with small spines. The young of the species have a rubbery texture, while adults are more flaccid.
The mouth is powerful and equipped with two large adjacent dental plates on each jaw. The coloring is typically mottled. In the young, the belly is marked by pronounced black stripes. The base of the pectoral fins is black. This fish propels itself along with its dorsal and anal fins. It is common to encounter this species on the sandy bottoms of lagoons. It grows to a length of 100-120 centimeters.

▶

DIODONTIDAE FAMILY

Burrfish
Diodon hystrix

◀ Tapered body, rounded toward the front, with large sharp spines which generally have split bases. Thes spines stand erect when the animal puffs up. The mouth has a single dental plate for each jaw. The snout and tail are elongated. The brownish-yellow coloring is fairly dark, with numerous black spots on the sides and the back. Nocturnal by habit, it seeks out sheltered places during the day. It is common, and in certain areas a diver may encounter dozens in a single dive. This fish grows to a length of ninety centimeters.

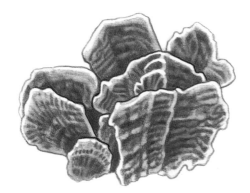

CNIDARIANS

Fire coral
Millepora platyphylla

◀ Despite its name, fire coral belongs to the class of hydrozoans and not anthozoans like true corals. Colonies of this type of fire coral are laminar and sinuate, and in general run parallel to each other. The surface is dotted with small conical protuberances. Up to sixty centimetres tall.

Branched fire coral
Millepora dichotoma

This is the colonial, arborescent species, with branches which regularly separate at the tips. They are also characteristically white. Fire corals are usually associated with symbiotic algae (*Zooxanthellae*), which explains its particular abundance in surface waters. Up to one meter in size.

▶

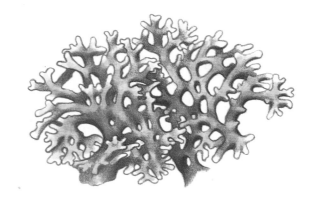

Soft corals
Dendronephtya sp.

◀ Soft corals are arborescent colonial organisms with various-sized branches. The branches are dotted with groups of polyps. The colonies consist of an elastic, translucent skeleton that reveals the calcareous spicules within. Soft corals expand at night, doubling in size. Up to one meter in size.

Giant anemone
Heteractis magnifica

This is a large anemone consisting of a blunt column from which run concentric lines of cylindrical tentacles, which also extend from the rounded tip. Its fuchsia or red outer color is characteristic and becomes evident when the anemone is contracted. It is associated with the clown anemonefish *Amphiprion bicinctus*. The sea anemone is common in well-illuminated surface waters.

▶

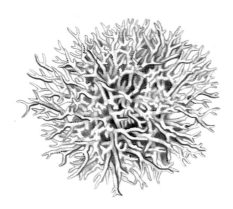

Porcupine coral
Seriatopora hystrix

◀ This coral forms bush-like, thickly branched colonies. The branches intersect and always end in a pointed spine. The polyps are visible at night. Lives in waters at depths of between three and twenty-five to thirty meters. Up to thirty centimeters in size.

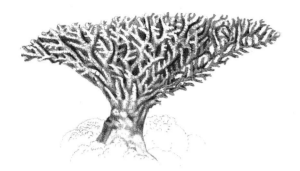

Acropora coral
Acropora sp.

◀ This is the most common genus of hard corals, with a form that may vary, depending on habitat and depth, from compact to branched to plate-shaped. In general, these corals grow rapidly, occupying vast areas of the sea bed. The small polyps open primarily at night. Plate acropora corals may reach two meters in diameter.

Leaf coral
Pachyseris sp.

Leaf corals form colonies in a flat leaf shape and may exceed two meters in diameter. The surface is interspersed with raised, parallel dissepiments in a concentric pattern. The calyxes are indistinct. In general, it colonizes hard, flat substrata at depths of between eight and sixty to seventy meters. The polyps are quite small and almost invisible.

Mushroom coral
Fungia sp.

◀ This coral has a characteristic disk or oval shape with raised and radial dissepiments that resemble the lamellae of a mushroom cap. It is the only non-colonial coral and only attaches itself to the seabed during its early phases. Its polyps have very mobile tentacles which can clean the surface of sediments. It is up to thirty centimeters in diameter.

Honeycomb coral
Favites sp.

Forms colonies in the shape of massive cushions. The corallites are often fused together, with raised walls intersected by transversal dissepiments which create a characteristic honeycomb pattern. The polyps are tube-shaped and expand primarily at night. Up to fifty centimeters in size.

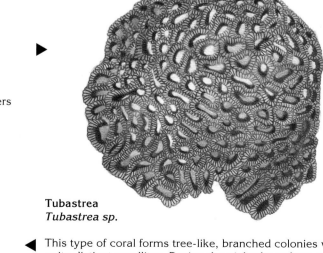

Tubastrea
Tubastrea sp.

◀ This type of coral forms tree-like, branched colonies with large, quite distinct corallites. During the night the polyps expand, showing their yellow and orange tentacles. In general, tubastrea grows in shadowy areas, due in part to the absence of symbiotic algae in its tissues. Can exceed fifty centimeters in size.

WORMS

Christmas tree worm
Spirobranchus giganteus

◀ This is a polychaete, sedentary worm that usually lives associated with the corals that cover it and protect its calcareous tube, from which sprouts a double branchial spiral-shaped tuft in which the operculum closing off the tube can be seen. Its color may vary, but is always vivid. Up to seven centimeters in size.

CRUSTACEANS

Cleaner shrimp
Stenopus hispidus

This is one of the most typical tropical cleaner shrimp, and can be recognized by its whitish body with broad red transversal bands. Its long, mobile white antennae are used to call fish to be cleaned. Up to six-seven centimeters in size.

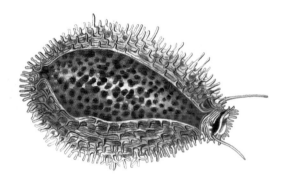

MOLLUSKS

Cowrie
Cypraea sp.

◀ The cowrie is a gastropod with an ovoid shell which is quite shiny due to the action of the well-developed mantle that surrounds and protects it. The upper portion is convex, while the lower part is flat. During the day it hides among the corals, where it camouflages itself by expanding its mantle. It feeds on algae and small benthic creatures.

Textile cone shell
Conus textile

This gastropod mollusk has a bi-conical, whorled, moderately high shell with long, narrow openings. The surface is smooth and shiny, with a characteristic pattern of dark transverse lines. This is a nocturnal species that will even hunt fish, killing them with its poisonous darts, which are potentially dangerous to humans as well. Up to ten-twelve centimeters in size.

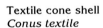

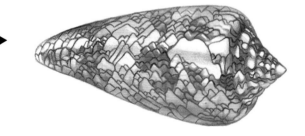

Sea triton
Charonia tritonis

◀ Large mollusk with a sturdy shell which develops into large spires that terminate in a blunt point. The opening is wide, permitting the red mollusk with its large foot to come out. This species feeds primarily on echinoderms, and is the principal predator of the crown-of-thorn starfish. Up to forty centimeters in size.

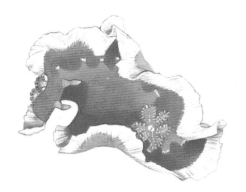

Spanish dancer
Hexabranchus sanguineus

◀ This is one of the largest and most showy nudibranchs in the Red Sea. It is unmistakable due to its bright color, often brilliant red, and the wide mantle that allows it to swim. On its dorsal and back portion is a clearly visible yellow gill, where symbiotic shrimp can often be seen. Up to forty centimeters in length.

Giant clam
Tridacna maxima

This large bivalve mollusc is one of the most well-known organisms of the coral reef. Its valves are thick and wavy. Inside is a fleshy colorful mantle which contains two openings that function as siphons and allow the animal to breathe and eat. The mantle's bright color is due to the presence of *Zooxanthellae*. Up to forty-fifty centimeters in size.

▶

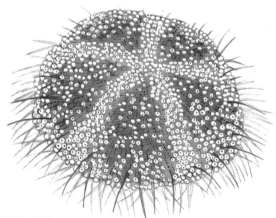

Pincushion urchin
Astenosoma varium

◀ This sea urchin is easily recognizable by the globular growths that surround the shorter spines; these are poisonous glands that accentuate the action of its stings. The shell is strangely flexible and will flatten if the animal is removed from the water. Up to fifteen centimeters in size.

ECHINODEMS

Crown-of-thorns starfish
Acanthaster plancii

This is the famous coral-devouring starfish which in the past has invaded vast areas of the tropical reefs. It can be recognized by its numerous sturdy arms (from ten to twenty-two), armed with strong spines covered with a toxic mucous. The starfish is more active at night, while during the day it tends to remain hidden. Up to forty centimeters in size.

▶

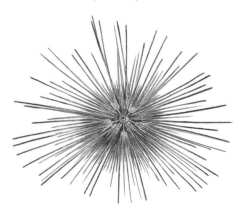

Long-spined urchin
Diadema setosum

◀ The distinguishing feature of the long-spined urchin is its long, thin stings, which are extremely mobile due to the strong muscles at their base. It is nocturnal, and by day tends to take refuge in the darker areas of the reef. Its stings are painful. Up to twenty-thirty centimeters in size.

168 Sea turtles (Chelonia midas) are a common sight during explorations of the Red Sea's floor. These peaceful reptiles are primarily carnivores, with a diet that includes jellyfish, cuttlefish and other small fish.

The author would like to thank Fulvia Lami, Luca Frigo and the whole staff of the HOLIDAY SERVICE diving school and everyone whose valuable assistance contributed to the creation of this guide.

Special thanks to Nadia Alzani, my patient and irreplaceable collaborator.